love your home

habitat

love your home
habitat

tamsin blanchard
foreword by tom dixon
special photography by kevin davies

conran OCTOPUS

04

First published in 2004 by Conran Octopus Limited
a part of Octopus Publishing Group
2–4 Heron Quays, London E14 4JP
www.conran-octopus.co.uk

British Library Cataloguing-in-Publication Data.
A catalogue record for this book is available from
the British Library.

ISBN 1 84091 374 6

Printed in China

Publishing Director *Lorraine Dickey*
Art Director *Chi Lam*
Executive Editor *Zia Mattocks*
Book Design *Untitled*
Editor *Sian Parkhouse*
Picture Research Manager *Liz Boyd*
Picture Researcher *Anne-Marie Hoines*
Special Photography *Kevin Davies*
Production Manager *Angela Couchman*

love your home

create 10

indulge 20

dress 66

share 116

imagine 168

index 202
habitat store directory 206
acknowledgments 208

foreword
tom dixon

'Love your home' is not a wishy-washy sentiment or a command, but a rallying call, a manifesto for all of us who believe that home is where the heart is. After all, where we live is central to our wellbeing. While the Modernist manifesto which claimed that the home of the future was destined to become a 'machine for living' was visionary for its time, it is probably time for us to think of the house as more than the sum of its parts.

In the twenty-first century, we need a dwelling to be more than a place for sleeping and eating, more than just an investment in property, more than just a shelter from the elements. We need to imbue it with all sorts of mysterious qualities – things such as comfort and history, flexibility and warmth – for it to become the refuge we need from an aggressive and chaotic life outside. We want it to work as the social hub for our family, but also need it to take on extra flexibility as our lives become more fragmented, as work and marriage are no longer institutions for life but more like temporary states of being, with all kinds of complex, unclassifiable arrangements in between. Kids stay at home longer as housing costs spiral out of young people's reach. The previously clear distinctions between work and rest become increasingly blurred, with computerization and globalization allowing or forcing people to work from any space available. Even institutions such as 'breakfast' vanish in place of a banana while getting dressed, a cappuccino in a paper cup on the bus, or a bottle of water on the desk.

Other pressures appear in the eternal battle for space. We need our homes to hold more stuff as we acquire more new possessions – 500 CDs, the latest fashions, speciality cookware – but at the same time we do not want to get rid of our classic vinyl, our vintage jeans or our chicken brick. We want more gadgets and technology to make our lives more efficient, but we also want more Game Boys and flat-screen televisions, printers and scanners, lawn mowers and juicers. The home is put under increased stress from all these demands and, as a result, people are forced to reach into restricted attic spaces or dig deep into cellars, like primitive man seeking shelter. Yet while we want all these things, we also dream of a parallel universe, of a serene and tranquil rustic charm which reminds us of simpler times, or a minimalist pared-down environment that we have seen in the brochure of a luxury hotel chain.

These contradictions are the stuff of which the modern house is made up; they are the complexities that designers and architects worry about, that magazine editors and television researchers all look at and, ultimately, the thing that all of us confront when we get through our front door.

This, then, is the departure point for calling this book *Love Your Home*. Perhaps we can show how people deal with some of these challenges, and you can find inspiration in tips from others, be they gurus or professionals or just talented ordinary folk. But that's not all. We also want to find out how other people love their homes – by reinventing them or using them as inspiration for their art, or maybe even by building their own. We want to find out the tricks from the experts. We want to examine the things we use to stack and store, and clean and light our homes, and discover new ways to do it all better. We want to find out how people live, to poke our noses into their spaces and find out what inspires them. And, above all, to try to discover what tomorrow's habitat might look like.

love your home

Tom Dixon, creative director, Robin Day's Forum armchair from Habitat
'I live in a state of dissatisfaction like most people. I want my home to be vast but affordable. I want period charm and I demand the latest technology. I'd love a rural view, but I need a location with city-centre energy. I have to have a shed to mess about in at the bottom of the garden, but I'm desperate to live in a tower. Maybe it's a bit greedy, but I wouldn't mind a helicopter pad and central locking. That's why I live in a Victorian conversion like everyone else!'

10

love 6

create your home

indulge 20

dress 66

share 116

imagine 168

On 11 May 1964, Terence Conran opened Habitat. There was a party in the store on London's Fulham Road, and the great and the good and the beautiful – the Chelsea set – were all there. It didn't take long for word to spread. Here was a whole new way of shopping – a store that sold not just affordable, modern furniture, but everything you might need for a bright new home.

In postwar Britain, most people's homes were drab, dreary and functional. Furniture was dark and heavy. Carpets and wallpapers were traditional. Curtains (drapes) blocked light from the windows. 'Bathrooms,' recalls Conran, 'were like prison cells. You went into ridiculous front rooms – decorated with wedding gifts – that you never used except for births and deaths.' The bright new optimism that had been sweeping through the country since the ending of postwar rationing, and the futuristic Festival of Britain, had yet to reach most people's homes. They might have given their wardrobes a bit of a pep-up, with short skirts and stretchy fabrics. Architects might have been leading the way in their open-plan Hampstead pads, but the fresh breeze of modernity had not quite arrived in the average living room. But Habitat was to change all that.

Terence Conran was trained as a textile designer at Central School of Arts and Crafts, but he had a much wider vision that was to encompass the way we lived. When he became a furniture designer, he wasn't interested in a chair in isolation. He wanted to give people a whole new environment. When Habitat opened its doors, this little island became part of something bigger, brighter, sunnier and – most importantly – more continental. There were red-and-white checked tablecloths like those in French bistros. There were continental quilts like the ones people slept under in Sweden; new lamps and lights like the Italians used; and colourful prints fresh from Finland.

The bag reads:

habitat

KITCHEN GOODS FABRICS CARPETS CHINA & GLASS FURNITURE

AT THE JUNCTION OF SLOANE AVENUE & FULHAM ROAD

THEIR INFLUENCE ON YOUR HOME

YOUNG MAN LEADING A FURNITURE REVOLUTION

It juts like a gleaming glass-and-brick promontory into the architectural confusion of London's Fulham Road. From each of its 13 plate glass windows, foot-high white letters proclaim the name: Habitat.

To a casual, uninformed by-passer this might seem to be just another slick, expensive shop selling slick, expensive furniture. But to designer Terence Conran, Habitat's fou[nder] and director, this store is much [more] than that. 'We aim to provide [a] complete look in furnishing, a [range] of high-style household kit a[t the] lowest possible cost—which ca[n] be seen under one roof.'

Still only months old, Habitat i[s the] result of Conran's shrewd obse[rva]tion that, while today's young ne[eds]

56

'A treasure trove of the best in modern furniture, china, glass and kitchen equipment.' The director, Terence Conran, shown here in the basement of his shop, Habitat.

by
ANNE BARRIE

photograph by
Michael Irwin

No 1   TERENCE CONRAN

veds will spend money on making hemselves look 'absolutely super' hey often neglect the surroundings n which they live. The reason, he naintains, is that until now it has een difficult to create a lively, panking-bright home without pending a mint of money, or undereaking the perpetual burden of hire urchase payments. 'Young people

simply won't saddle themselves with enormous HP debts early in their married life. I spent a lot of time thinking about this, trying to decide what sort of kit we could give them which would make even the most monstrously dismal flat or small house look good, on the least amount of money. Habitat is our answer.' To provide his answer, Terence Con-

ran has amassed an impressive array of household goods from most of Britain's top designers. In the store's airy, grey-carpeted interior, simple bentwood and cane chairs flank deep, plushy sofas; sturdy dining tables in scrubbed natural pine are set with enamel mugs, a bright red coffee pot; bolts of fabric sit, easy to see and to feel, on shallow

57

right First introduced in 1965 as a mail-order tool, the catalogue soon became a coffee-table favourite. Its mission: 'Conran furniture is designed to match the mood of present-day living.'

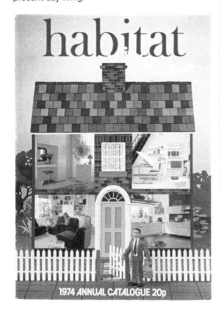

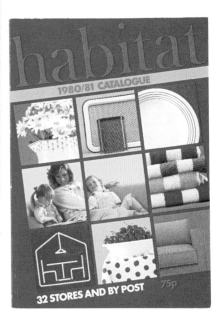

The first store, on London's fashionable Fulham Road, was a whole new shopping experience. 'I'd been terrifically influenced by going round French markets,' Conran explains. 'And I liked that generosity – the availability of it – where you just take it off the shelf and put it in a basket and take it up to the cash till. It was a real eye-opener to me. I saw in rural France the sort of life I thought I'd like to live and came back to grey, dreary rationed Britain and there were none of the pleasures I had experienced – the markets, the shops, the cafés, the *joie de vivre*. I felt a sort of educational urge to say, "Look, you can have this."'

He applied the way French market stalls stacked their goods to his furniture and household accessories. It fitted in with his egalitarian take on offering good design to all. 'I think it communicated itself fairly rapidly. There were those genteel ladies who came in in the early days and said to the shop assistants, "Could I have one of those, do you think?" And the shop assistant would say, "Well, I'll give you a basket and you go and take what you want."'

Habitat was never going to be just another snooty, rarefied showroom. It was designed to be a bustling place, with huge windows out on to the world. And it appealed to a wide range of shoppers – from Conran's architect and artist friends to other designers, as well as some famous faces from the local Chelsea set, including models Jean Shrimpton and Twiggy, and George Harrison and Peter

Sellers. It was a place, as they say, to see and be seen, the interiors equivalent of Barbara Hulanicki's celebrated Biba fashion boutique just down the road.

The concept was ahead of its time. It remains virtually unchanged to this day – right down to the original logo. The name, incidentally, came from *Roget's Thesaurus*. Conran's friend, the model Pagan Taylor, was looking up other words for home. Habitat leapt out as the obvious choice. The dictionary definition of habitat is 'the natural home of an organism'. And it was all about creating a natural habitat for people to feel at home. 'Really, the point of Habitat was could we be bothered to go on trying to sell domestic furniture or should we go back to doing contract furniture? So I said let's open a shop to show people how it could be done. So that was Habitat. One of the ideas was that furniture was the main thing that was sold, but one of the things I had noticed going round all the shops was how empty they were, so we tried to sell all the other things that go into making a house. I was very influenced by Elizabeth David. There was French and Italian kitchen equipment and bits of lighting and textiles and china and glass. I looked around for things that were quite plain and simple, but that had some style to them. That's really how it came about.'

Conran makes it sound almost accidental, but Habitat was the first real 'lifestyle' store, putting its products – the flat-pack furniture, the glasses and the lighting – in a wider

right The catalogue was influential in giving the consumer a look to which they could aspire. Sometimes, Conran would use the homes of his friends to display his new furniture and accessories.

context. With its annual catalogues, which quickly became coffee-table must-haves, it was as aspirational as it was inspirational. It took the whole area of design to a broader market. It was no longer the preserve of black poloneck-clad, espresso-drinking architects and their friends. And people began to look at their homes in terms of fashion, rather than simply function. They could dress their beds in bright new sheets and quilt covers; hide their stained old dining tables under colourful new tablecloths; change their lampshades as often as their shoes.

Alongside the fashionable accessories, designed to brighten and update your home for a few seasons, Habitat has also always provided items that are simply good at what they do. Conran introduced them because they were fantastic examples of good design – sometimes things he had seen on his frequent travels in France. They have a natural honesty and integrity that made them necessary, rather than fashionable. They were things people knew they could count on, no matter what new innovations were being sold alongside them. For Conran, it was perhaps just an instinctive feel for what was Habitat. The pepper grinder like the ones they used in the local Italian pizzeria, or the café-style Duralex wine glasses – these were all part of the unique Habitat mix. When Tom Dixon became design director in 1999, he identified these objects and gave them a name. He called them 'archetypes'.

'An archetype is almost like the object a kid would draw,' explains Dixon. 'You know, if you said draw me a chair, or draw me a lampshade, it would be that. It's a memory of an object – the obvious one.' For him, archetypes are the objects you see in cartoon strips, such as the galvanized metal garbage cans in *Top Cat*. They are almost caricatures of themselves. His job is occasionally to give the object a twist, to make it Habitat. It will usually be a matter of simply changing its colour, or using a different material.

These items are iconic. There is a certain satisfaction about them in that you recognize them from your grand-mother's kitchen or living room. They have been around for ever and have a tremendous comforting appeal. They are innately conservative. 'But those objects still have a place,' says Dixon. 'You can guarantee that if a spaceman living in a space station had the choice, he would bring a couple of his cultural memories with him – he'd have a gilt frame with a picture of his grandma or his baby.

'When Terence was doing it, it was more a matter of him saying, "I just like this because it works",' says Dixon. Then, the Van Gogh rush-seated kitchen chairs looked fresh and new. They also did a job very well. But 40 years on, Dixon wanted to separate the innovations from the non-innovations. 'I wanted to try to force the designers into a position where what they were designing was really pushing the boundaries and just letting go of all the other

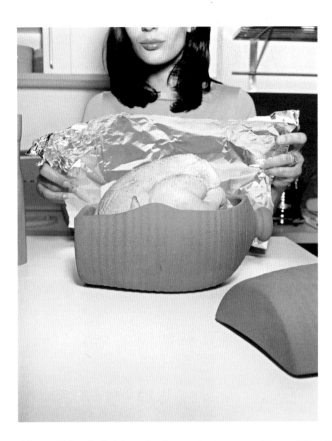

things. This whole idea of trying to design everything a little bit more was counterproductive in my view. You're killing yourself trying to design something that exists already, that is really good and looks like a Habitat product, when you should be killing yourself trying to think of something new that has never been seen before. We have a massive turnover of ideas. There are 5,000 items in the range. Why bother with things that are perfect? Anything that you do actually spoils it, when you should be doing something that covers the halogen bulb, for example, because that's new technology; there's no shade that does that job properly.'

Some things simply cannot be improved upon. The Brown Betty teapot is as traditional and classic a design as they come. Dixon even goes so far as to question its relevance in the twenty-first century. 'There is no reason to have a teapot in the modern world really – it's a ritual. Everybody really has a tea bag and a mug. In some senses the teapot is redundant. But it still does a job.' If you want to have your in-laws round for afternoon tea, you might want to think about getting the best china out, or at least a fancy tea cosy. But if you are old-fashioned, and like to make your tea the proper way (rather than in a mug with a tea bag), it cannot be bettered. 'Are you the kind of person that wants your teapot to look like a rocket ship, or a Hoover, or a designed object?' asks Dixon. 'Or do you want it to have that humble non-designed classic feel?

It's one of the toughest briefs to make a new teapot that doesn't drip and that you can hold without the lid falling off – and that one does the job.' It is anti-design. Some of these items are beyond design. They just are.

As well as being 'intelligent' products, there is a certain amount of knowingness and irony about some of Dixon's archetypes. Such as the chesterfield sofa. Habitat's version of the old classic comes in black and red. It is shiny and new. When used in the right environment, it serves as a nod to all the beaten-up old chesterfields that inhabit institutions from the gentlemen's club to the local bar. For Dixon, it is just another component to your own landscape.

These archetypal products have stood the test of time; many have not consciously been designed at all. Their form has simply followed their function. Their form has evolved naturally, totally without artifice. They have not been sculpted out of Styrofoam to within a millimetre of their most ergonomic shape. They did not even start life on a drawing board. They are the workhorses of the home around which everything else falls into place. For both Dixon and Conran it was – and still is – about making the world a better place through design. 'Most of us had this Bauhaus idea in our heads that if something was intelligently designed and priced at a price most people could afford, they might like it and buy it,' says Conran. 'What I was trying to do was say look at this, if you like it, well you can afford it, too.'

Habitat escalates to Tottenham Court Road, and opens a shining new furnishing and kitchen shop. So if you want to corner a cupboard, cook a carp or cut out some curtains zip along to Habitat 156-158 Tottenham Court Road London W1 EUS 3242 between Heals and Maples. Open all day Saturday. Late night Thursday. Normally closed Mondays but open for Christmas shoppers Monday 5th 12th 19th December. And also 77 Fulham Road London SW7 KEN 3277 of course.

habitat escalates

20

love 6

create 10

indulge your home

dress 66

share 116

imagine 168

right Having a lie-in
at the weekend can be
the ultimate in domestic
luxury – especially
when your bed is a
haven of eiderdowns
and fluffy pillows.

Your home is your escape, your comfort zone. It might be crammed full of your favourite things. Or it might be stripped bare. You might like it warm and soothing. You may prefer your surroundings cool and industrial. It might be light; it might be dark. Everyone's idea of a secret refuge away from the world outside is different. But however we choose to feather it, we all love to have a nest to go home to at the end of the day.

Home is a place we can spoil ourselves. We can sit and watch the football with a can of beer. We can dress up (or down) to suit ourselves. We can lounge around in a pair of sweat pants. We can snooze in a kaftan. We can paint our nails. We can play music and read a book. We can soak in the bath for hours on end. We can put our feet up. We can make a mess. We can do what we want. Our homes are where we can indulge ourselves and our families. But with the rigours and demands of modern life, most of us rarely have the chance. We wake up late, have a quick shower, grab a coffee for breakfast and run for the bus. We get home late, eat a quick meal in front of the television and go to bed, ready to start all over again the next day. Everything is rushed. And by the end of the week, our homes are chaos zones, with piles of dirty laundry, overflowing rubbish bins, unopened mail, clothes scattered about and nothing to eat or drink in the refrigerator. We spend our weekends out and about to avoid the mess back home. We go on expensive holidays so that we can get away from our chaotic lives. But it doesn't have to be like this.

Learning to love your home is just a matter of spending more time there. Don't try to escape from it – escape *to* it. And if your home is a mess, do something about it. Look after it just as you look after yourself. If you approach them the right way, even household chores can be a pleasure. Certainly, the way we clean our homes has come a long way since our grandparents' days. It's no longer necessary

'My home is my true, true refuge from life and work. As soon as I close my door it is me; this is what a home should be! My favourite place in my house? My George Sherlock reading chair in my study. I love to be surrounded by my books that I adore. When I am reading is the only time I can really relax – I am totally gone; I lose all sense of time. This is my haven.'

Manolo Blahnik, shoe designer

to get down on your hands and knees, with your hair tied up in a turban and a housecoat on to protect your dress, to scrub the floor. High-tech vacuum cleaners; computer-programmed washing machines; brightly coloured brushes that look like works of art; glamorous feather dusters and shiny stainless-steel dustpan-and-brush sets all make maintaining your home fun rather than an effort. Don't just pamper yourself – pamper your home, too.

With the right care and attention, even the most humble abode has the potential to be a palace. Home, as they say, is where the heart is. It's all about making the mundane marvellous. The most basic things can be luxurious in their own way. If you clean a milk bottle and fill it with daffodils, it becomes so simple and personal, it's charming.

It is a matter of presentation. An old, stained tea towel that has seen better days can make your kitchen look depressing and grim. A crisp new one with a bright pattern or an interesting design will give your kitchen the look of somewhere cool and dynamic. A beaten-up old saucepan will make you think of school dinners, while a sleek, shiny, stainless-steel one will elevate your cookery to something altogether more fabulous. Democracy of design means the most basic things should be as well thought through as the more fanciful ones. If everything in your life is well designed, from the teaspoon you use to stir your coffee to the broom you use to sweep the floor, your life should be easier and more enjoyable. It will certainly look better.

It is the everyday items that make a difference to our lives. Sometimes, all it takes is a sideways glance to make something out of the ordinary. Using a basic material to make something remarkable is as effective as taking an expensive material and making something simple. It works both ways. There is no reason why a frame made of plastic shouldn't have the curlicues and grandeur of a frame made out of gilt. And just because a blanket is plain wool, why not add sparkle? With a little know-how and imagination, you can customize your basics yourself. It's an idea borrowed from the world of fashion. You don't have to spend a million dollars to look it. Make cushion covers out of exotic fabrics – velvet and silk – and pile them high like a maharajah. Sprinkle sequins across an old bedspread.

Making something from nothing is an art in itself. Some designers pride themselves on their ability to do it. Martino Gamper and Rainer Spehl are London-based designers who make magic with other people's rubbish. They are always on the lookout for broken bits of furniture, left in skips (dumpsters) or abandoned on street corners. They call it 'furniture while you wait' and will customize old junk into something challenging or useful, or simply something you hadn't thought of before. The most banal thing can be beautiful, whether it is a stack of plastic electrical ties, a cardboard food container, a coat hanger or a paper doily. For Royal Collage of Art graduate Tim Parsons, the challenge is to make the ordinary extraordinary. His Turned

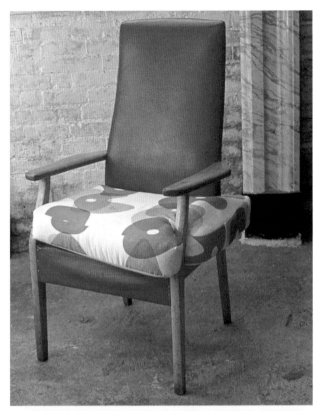

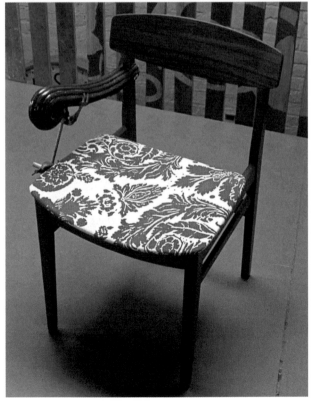

Candle is a basic wax candle carved to look as though it has been traditionally turned like an antique table leg. His woven wicker coat hanger is a piece of fine craftsmanship.

The point is, making your home into something luxurious and comfortable doesn't mean you have to be a millionaire. If you pay attention to the finer details, everything else will follow. A glamorous home is one that is filled with personal touches. It might be a matter of keeping your Christmas decorations out all year round (some people do), or at least making some fairy lights a permanent feature of your living space. In the 1970s, you couldn't get more glamorous than the home of the restaurateur Mr Chow. And what made his London pad so fabulous? The Chinese paper kites he had pinned to the walls. They probably cost pennies from Chinatown (and still do). If you collect stuff, find ways of displaying it. Show off your silk kimonos. Hang up your vintage lace dresses. Make a gallery of your postcards. If you hate clutter, find ways of storing it so that your home is full of clean lines and elegant spaces.

Be selective about what you put in your home. Make each and every thing count. Some of the great designs of the twentieth century are still in production, from Kenneth Grange's 1960s Mariner clock to Henry Massonnet's 1968 plastic Tam Tam stool. And – true to their designers' initial visions – they remain as accessible and affordable today as always. So go on, whether it is a tea towel or an ashtray, indulge yourself. Indulge your home. You both deserve it.

left Making something out of nothing: Martino Gamper and Rainer Spehl give some old scrapheap finds a little tender loving care to make them new and relevant again.

right JAM uses recycled cylinders from washing machines to make shiny storage units.

first impressions

right Carl Clerkin and Gitta Gschwendter's Hidden hallway unit gives a full-length mirror hidden depths.

far right Organization in the form of shoe racks, coat hooks and shelving is the key to a smart, uncluttered hallway.

First impressions really do count. If the first thing you see when you walk into a house is a messy, unloved hallway, it will colour your view of everything else you see. Halls and entrance areas often serve as storage space and cloak-rooms, and quickly become a dumping ground for coats, shoes, umbrellas, bags, and such like. But systemization and some cleverly designed furniture are all it takes to transform a mess into a marvel. Sometimes it is simply a matter of putting up a set of hooks. A magnetic board for keys is also a good place to start – you'll always know where they are. A new doormat is cheap to buy, but makes a big difference to the overall impression you create. And a neat shoe rack will help you keep the floor free from clutter. If you allow too much junk to accumulate in your hallway, the space will feel as though it is closing in on you. But if your hallway is pristine, light and airy, it will give the illusion that the rest of your home is like that too.

When Gitta Gschwendter and Carl Clerkin set about making useful hallway furniture, they came up with a mirror unit called Hidden. As well as a vertical box for your mobile (cell) phone and a horizontal one for letters and papers, it features two hooks for keys. When you come home from work, you can offload the things you might normally leave on a table or scatter around the home in one logical place. And in the morning before you go to work, you can check in the mirror that you are not still wearing your slippers, or give your hair a last-minute tidy.

making the ordinary extraordinary

Whenever you see homes that have been photographed for glossy magazines, they always seem to be filled with perfect flower arrangements. This is because all stylists know the magic a bunch of flowers can work in a room. They can distract from dark corners, uninteresting shelves and horrible furniture. They can also make a space look as though it is cared for and loved. They can add an instant injection of glamour. It needn't be an extravagant display of luscious lilies, rampant roses or oriental orchids. A simple of bunch of daffodils in springtime will do the trick. More important than the flowers, however, is the vase.

In Japan, flower arranging is still considered to be a part of a girl's education. For some, it is a reason to rebel. For others, it is just as good a reason to dry out a few empty gourds; they make the most exquisite vases. Simple things can make seriously glamorous vessels, whether for flowers or as objects in their own right. British design team JAM collaborated with Philips, and took the lowly light bulb and made it into a fragile vase. For the recycled-glass company TransGlass, it was the wine bottle. They slice the top off and grind and polish the edges to make something pure, modern and almost unrecognizable from its origins. And then there are the test-tube clusters designed by French design duo Tsé & Tsé.

Catherine Lévy and Sigolène Prébois met at design school in Paris and eventually began working together as Tsé & Tsé, creating fun and quirky products. Their lighting, in particular, is more decorative than functional, and their floral lighting arrangement for Habitat is more like an art installation than something you would hang around your Christmas tree. Fairy lights have undergone a radical transformation over the past decade. No longer simply for Christmas, they have transcended the kitsch to become a decorative feature all of their own. Ever since Corinne Day photographed Kate Moss with a simple string of lights taped to the wall behind her for British *Vogue* magazine, they have become every home's coolest decorative accessory. For fairground gaudiness, choose bright colours or, if you like things a little more ethereal, go for plain white, with a delicate flower-shaped shade.

One of the simplest ways to indulge your home is with cushions and throws made out of luxurious fabrics. Silk, velvet and cashmere add an extravagance to any room. You can either buy them – new or second-hand – or look out for fabrics that you can make up yourself. Old velvet drapes are always a good buy, as aged velvet has that look of an instant heirloom. And vintage throws, patchwork quilts and satin eiderdowns for beds and sofas will simply make everyone believe you had a very rich and fabulous grandmother. If your blanket collection is more basic, you can always lavish them with trimmings. Keep an eye out in haberdashery departments for ribbons and tassels. Knit cushion covers out of cashmere, and add a sprinkle of sequins to an old blanket for a home fit for a magpie.

twinkle twinkle

Fairy lights are an instant glamour fix. Simply plug them in, and trail them along the floor. They are also very effective arranged on a wall as a piece of art – like the stem of a flower, or in zigzags, circles or a random pattern. Using masking tape to fix your string of lights to the wall gives a rough and ready look, or you can use small cable clips. Drape them around your windows or picture frames; for extra sparkle, hang them around a mirror above a fireplace. You can also wind them around a staircase, or make them into a heart shape for over your bed. Turn other lights down low and just enjoy the mood.

making the ordinary extraordinary 31

left Milk bottles and other everyday glass containers can be elevated into charming vases with some simple flower arranging.

right Tsé & Tsé's test-tube vases are on display on a kitchen counter at their home in Paris.

on display

_ Anything looks good in quantity – toys, Action Men, record or CD covers, Russian dolls, wooden ducks or anything else for which you might nurture a secret passion.
_ Mix and mis-match old china plates and cups and saucers from junk stores and pretend they are family heirlooms.
_ Make your own mini works of art. Frame postcards or your favourite swatch of fabric, or even a small square of a wallpaper that catches your eye.
_ Give an old sofa a new lease of life with a glamorous throw. Look out for antique quilts at flea markets.

making the mundane marvellous

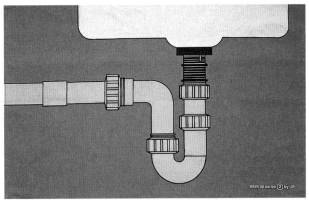

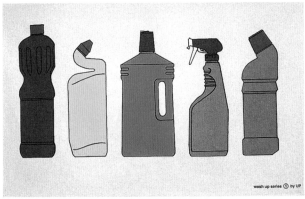

Some people enjoy cleaning their homes. Really, they do. They get immense satisfaction out of scrubbing the floors, polishing the furniture and even cleaning the toilet. These are the sort of people who actually take great pleasure in choosing the right brush, cloth or bucket for a particular job. It's all about taking pride in our homes, from the utility items and tools that keep our floors clean or our windows sparkling, to the very containers that hold our rubbish.

Take the humble toilet brush. Who would have thought it would be the focus of so many designers' attentions? But shopping for a loo brush is a serious business these days. Your toilet deserves the best. And there it is, in all its finery, by Stefano Giovannoni, made for Italian company Magis. It's called the Merdolino, which sounds rude whatever language you use. His brief was to make the toilet brush fun, so he made it look like a child's toy in brightly coloured plastic. Or how about the dish drainer? Marc Newson's Dish Doctor makes doing the dishes all part of the fun. It comes in a whole array of colours (a different one for every day of the week) and has an integral reservoir for drips so that you can use it on your counter. Then there are Kartell plastic buckets (their kitchen steps are pretty cool, too), and – also by Stefano Giovannoni for Magis – brightly coloured brooms which come complete with matching hooks so you can hang them on the wall for everyone to see. Even the rubbish bin has been elevated to a work of

art. Habitat took the classic aluminium garbage can we know and love from the *Top Cat* cartoons and painted it a shiny shade of pillar-box red. It's almost too good to use.

Or how about transforming something as simple as the tea towel? We're not talking the sort you might find in a museum shop printed with a Picasso or a Mondrian painting (although these have certain kitsch appeal, and you should probably start collecting them now). These tea towels are quite specific and are made by a company called Unity Peg, the brainchild of furniture designer Jane Atfield and her artist husband Robert Shepherd. 'We wanted to explore visual ideas and create contemporary items that are accessible, useful and desirable within a domestic context,' they say. They aim to 'challenge the prosaic nature and low status of the tea towel'.

Even if you have no intention of cleaning, shopping for the equipment has never been more seductive. Gone are the days of the string mop and tin bucket (although they probably have a certain ironic utility chic about them). If it's functional, you can be sure someone has also made it fun. Habitat's stainless-steel dustpan-and-brush set has an air of nostalgia about it – the sort of thing the school janitor would have had in his store cupboards. Except, of course, his wouldn't have looked quite so shiny. These are cleaning implements you need to keep polished for the full effect. They're not just functional – they are part of the decoration.

left Graphic images used by the design company Unity Peg to elevate the lowly tea towel to must-have status include bottles of cleaning fluids, from bleach to washing-up liquid, and the U-bend of the sink.

right Household basics reinvented: Habitat's shiny steel dustpan and brush and the archetypal trash can painted glossy red.

how to care for wooden floors

_ Water and wood don't mix, so keep the floor dust- and dirt-free by regular vacuuming. Grit and dirt can cause scratches, so be vigilant. Use a damp mop if necessary.
_ Use baby oil to cover scratches.
_ Once a year, give your floor a wax.
_ Don't let visitors walk on the floors in stiletto heels. Buy glamorous slippers from Chinatown for them to use instead.
_ Use coasters and felt foot covers for heavy furniture.
_ When moving furniture, use heavy blankets, and place thick socks over feet that will scratch.

left Dish drainers come in all shapes and forms. This one almost has a touch of the Heath Robinson about it.

right Marc Newson's Dish Doctor almost makes washing the dishes fun.

far right These colourful brooms by Magis look like they would be more at home in a sweet shop (candy store) window than a kitchen.

affordable classics

Some of the best products have already been designed – often in the 1960s, when a whole generation of designers emerged who seemed to be on a mission to produce good design that was accessible to all. Robin Day, for example, was typical of his contemporaries in his genuine belief that good design could make the world a better place and, in support of this, he has spent most of his working life concentrating on making the simplest things in life work better, and look better. Often, these products were made in plastic, a material that revolutionized our lives in the twentieth century. Thankfully, many of those designs – which have never been bettered – are still in production.

In recognition of this wonderful legacy, Habitat launched its Twentieth-Century Legends Series in 1999. This was a collection of re-editions of products by some of the great names in design in the twentieth century, among them Robin and Lucienne Day, Verner Panton, Anna Castiglioni and Pierre Paulin. Many of the designers were into their seventies, but still working and as passionate about design as ever. 'Their work ethic was incredible,' says Tom Dixon, who went to meet many of them. And, of course, the work looked as modern and relevant at the brink of the twenty-first century as it did in when it was first produced in the 1960s. Some of the pieces, including the Castiglioni storage pods and Robin Day's Forum leather sofa and the 675 dining chair with arms like wings, have continued to be produced as staples of the Habitat range.

The Clam ashtray
Alan Fletcher designed the Clam ashtray in 1968 for the Italian company Mebel. The inspiration for the Clam had come to him while riding on a London bus one evening. The simplest ideas are often the best, and Fletcher was thinking about cheese – Edam cheese, in its shiny red waxy coat. The two identical halves of the Edam-shaped ashtray would be made from one mould and the serrated teeth would hold the halves firmly together, but also act as the perfect grip to a cigarette. Several cigarettes, in fact. The Clam, originally made from melamine, is two ashtrays in one – big enough to serve the needs of an entire party. And it is guaranteed to be a talking point, too.

Fletcher was a founding member, in 1972, of the ground-breaking London-based design company Pentagram. He trained at Central School of Arts and Crafts and the Royal College of Art in London, and Yale University School of Art, and is often inspired by everyday things such as cheese. He left Pentagram in 1992 to set up his own studio, working with clients including *Domus* magazine, London Transport, Shell and Toyota. 'If you have a solid concept,' he says, 'it has the potential to be timeless because it's not fixed to what's hot this month.' The Clam has proved this – it has been hot for almost 40 years and was treated to a new lease of life when it featured as part of the Twentieth-Century Legends series. The ashtray was reproduced in red and black, and looked as bold and graphic as ever.

The Tam Tam stool

Designed by Henry Massonnet in 1968, the Tam Tam stool was almost an accident. Massonnet, now in his eighties, first made it to go with the iceboxes he was producing at his plastics factory in Nurieux near the Swiss border in France. 'I designed it myself,' he says. 'It's a mathematical shape, a hyperbolic parallelepiped. We wanted the stool to be made of two identical parts that could be easily put together, so there weren't that many solutions. I didn't bother with lots of research. It seemed so obvious. I didn't have to rack my brains.' The Tam Tam, which can be easily dismantled and assembled, and is light enough for even a toddler to carry, will soon be celebrating its fortieth anniversary. With the exception of a blip in 1973 when production was curtailed by the oil crisis, the Tam Tam has never really been out of production. More than 12 million have been produced and sold worldwide.

At first, the stool didn't take off. But when a magazine published a story about French actress Brigitte Bardot, photographed in her home, complete with Tam Tam in her living room, a design icon was born. Production was stepped up, and they were made in a rainbow of colours. When Habitat started selling it in 2002, the stool's fortunes were revived. It is still made using the original mould. Massonnet, now in semi-retirement, is delighted.

The Mariner clock

You will undoubtedly have used one – if not several – of Kenneth Grange's products at some point in your life. Not only did he design the latest version of the famous London black taxicab, he worked on the InterCity 125 train, the Kodak Instamatic camera (it sold over 25 million worldwide after it was launched in 1968) and the Kenwood Chef food mixer, which is still in production, virtually unchanged from its original design in the late 1950s.

Like Alan Fletcher, Grange was a long-standing partner of Pentagram. 'If you are a designer, you have an obligation to the user,' he says. 'That means that the user has to enjoy what you do.' He formed his company, Kenneth Grange Designs, in 1958, working across the design fields of packaging, interiors, products and graphics.

The Mariner clock is typical of Grange's work in its apparently effortless pared-down simplicity and its strong graphic image. He designed it in the late 1960s for 'an old-fashioned firm making a variety of home instruments'. He says they wanted a modern version. And that is what they got. Grange has an incredible talent for making products that stand the test of time. 'They need to be decent value for money, they need to continuously look "of today" and they need to be in the portfolio of a business that is not a slave to the media and fashion trade,' he insists.

below left The Tam Tam stool is useful as a bedside table, a handy stool, in the garden, and can even be used as storage.

right Kenneth Grange's Mariner clock was designed in the 1960s, but with its graphic face and simple styling it remains timeless.

love your home

Melinda Ashton Turner, interior stylist and contributor to the Guardian, *with Lola, Mandarin light from Habitat*
'Space and light are the most important features to me. It doesn't matter how many gorgeous objects I surround myself with, I need these two qualities as the foundation around which I can build my home. Calmness in the layout and simplicity in colour and texture are the next priorities for me. I love objects made from everyday materials, and a piece such as the Mandarin light gives the room a focal point.'

archetype

blue and white cornish kitchenware
Despite its name, Cornish Kitchenware is not made in Cornwall. It is made by Thomas Goodwin Green pottery in South Derbyshire. The blue-and-white striped pots, jugs (pitchers) and mugs are largely unchanged in design and manufacture since they were first introduced in the 1920s. After World War I, and with glass taking over from earthenware beer mugs, times were hard for the pottery industry and it was forced to diversify. The pottery began to make storage jars in a traditional blue and white stripe, and eventually expanded into teapots, milk jugs and other utility kitchen items. The story goes that a salesman had returned from holiday in Cornwall and was inspired by the blue skies and white waves to call the range Cornish Kitchenware. The broad creamy white and sky blue stripes have been much copied ever since, but the real thing cannot be beaten. It was one of the first attempts to brighten up basic kitchen items for a mass market. Although it is still in production, original pieces from the 1920s and 1930s are now highly collectible.

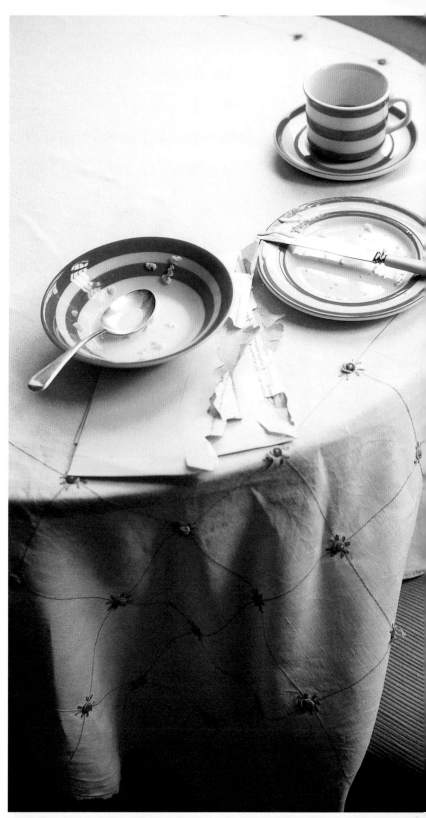

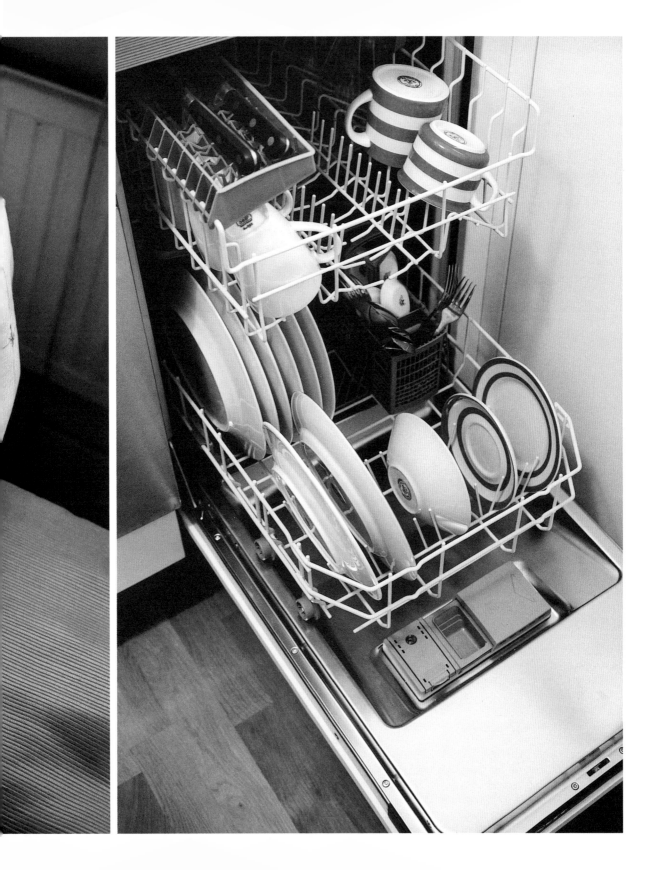

basic deluxe design

Robin Day is a designer with principles. From the outset, his products have had to be as cost-effective as they are functional. His stackable Polyprop chair, designed in 1962, is a perfect example of this democracy through design. It is functional, accessible, affordable and so ubiquitous as to have gone beyond 'design'. It is a basic item, but made in such a way that it is the best possible seating solution. The materials used are cheap. The manufacture is quick and easy – injection-moulded polypropylene on a bent steel base (the chair was one of the first pieces of furniture to utilize the mass-manufacturing potential of injection moulding). We've all sat on it – at school, in a waiting room or at work. Since 1963, the Polyprop has been so successful that we no longer even notice it. A staggering 14 million chairs have been sold in 23 different countries.

When Habitat started selling the Polyprop in 1999, it produced them in different colours – such as baby blue and translucent white – taking them out of their orange or grey plastic classroom context and into the home and the dining room. The chair became cherished, feted and even quite glamorous, rather than simply used and abused. It's still low cost, but that's not the reason people buy it for their homes. They buy it because it is as much an icon of design as the Arne Jacobsen Ant Chair or the Eames Lounger. It might not be so much of a status symbol, but it is just as good a piece of design. For Day, however, the chair has

served its purpose well. The fact that it had become so taken for granted was simply a sign of its success. He never intended it to be put on a pedestal.

Day, born in High Wycombe in 1915, is one of Britain's most influential designers. He graduated from the Royal College of Art in 1938 and married textile designer Lucienne Conradi in 1942. Six years later, they set up a design office specializing in graphic and industrial design and, in 1949, Day entered the international competition for low-cost furniture design held by the Museum of Modern Art in New York. He won first prize with his friend Clive Latimer for their elegant but simple plywood and tubular metal storage units, beating Charles Eames into second place. Until recently, the units had never been put into production, but Habitat saw the potential, and has been selling them since 2003. They look as fresh now as if designed last year.

'In my long years of designing,' Day told the *Guardian* in 1999, 'the thing that has always interested me is the social context of design and designing things that are good quality that most people can afford. In those days, and to some extent still today, furniture in high-street shops was not only not cheap, but it was also boring, conventional, semi-period and backward-looking. It was always my mission to mass-produce low-cost seating because I do think that clarity and what we call "good design" is a social force that can enhance people's environments.'

left and right Robin Day's humble Polyprop chair was originally designed for schools and waiting rooms, but it has been given a new lease of life in the home as a dining chair or as an extra armchair in the living room.

archetype

michael thonet's bentwood furniture

If the coat stand looks familiar, it is probably because you have hung your coat on it somewhere, if not in your own home, in a café, a bar or a restaurant. It was designed long before Habitat was even a twinkle in Terence Conran's eye, by the German furniture maker Michael Thonet. You will also be familiar with his bentwood chair; you must certainly have sat on one – possibly at your own kitchen table. Amazingly enough, the classic Number 14 chair, with its curvy back and round wickerwork seat, was the first industrially produced chair. It was designed in 1859 and is one of the most successful industrial products ever. The 50 millionth model came off the production line around about 1930, and is still going strong. It is made by steaming a piece of solid wood at very high temperatures; it is then bent by four men with strong clamps and immaculate timing. Each chair is different. The chair is a feat of simplicity, the back rest made up of just six components – two wooden rods, ten screws and two nuts.

The Number 14 inspired Thonet to produce a multitude of variations, including rocking chairs, armchairs and coat stands. Le Corbusier was a fan of the classic, wonderfully curvaceous 'Vienna' armchair. 'Never has anything been created more elegant and better in its conception, more precise in its execution, and more excellently functional.' Praise doesn't come much better than that.

bargain-hunting tip

Look out for Thonet bentwood chairs everywhere from junk shops, flea markets and charity stores to antiques sales. Made with either wickerwork or plywood seats, they are modern classics, but have become so popular that they can often be snapped up at bargain prices. It is possible to have broken wickerwork rewoven professionally – although that might cost more than the chair itself.

love your home

Dominic Lutyens, journalist,
Marcel coat stand from Habitat
'I love the fact there's lots of light and big windows, and being a loft apartment it's very practical. I like everything to be well finished, but unostentatious and simple. At the moment, it's all a bit neutral and I'd like to funk it up at some point (I'd love egg-yolk yellow kitchen units, in gloss). My furniture is retro a-go-go: 1960s apple-green plastic chair, 1970s Biba-esque sofa, Perspex coffee table and Eero Saarinen dining table, 1980s Memphis bookcase and, last but not least, my red Marcel coat stand.'

bright lights

Lighting continues to excite young designers, and it is the perfect arena for exploring new materials and technologies. Lampshades are a great vehicle for showcasing the latest materials – such as reflective foil, molten polystyrene or laser-etched metal – and they can drastically alter the mood and look of a room without great expense or effort.

Basic materials can be re-appropriated in the most unexpected of ways. Claire Norcross's Eightfifty light was made by accident. She was at the Museum of Science and Industry in Manchester after she had graduated from college, and says she 'accidentally dyed a cable tie'. She was looking at toothbrush fibres at the time, trying to make them into a light. 'I'm textile-based,' she says. Her degree was in embroidery, and she enjoys experimenting with fibres and materials. The ties used for the lamp are usually used in an industrial application. This is the first time they have been used to make something so bright and beautiful. But this was about re-appropriating materials, rather than recycling them in an ecological sense. 'The eco side wasn't my concern,' she says. Originally, she dyed the ties in a multitude of colours. But for mass production for Habitat, they are sprayed. The result is quite unlike anything else you have ever seen – tactile, unusual and sure to become a talking point in any room.

For Paul Cocksedge, the humble polystyrene coffee cup was the starting point for a series of Styrene lampshades. His first experiments began at the Royal College of Art, by exposing polystyrene cups to heat. 'They seemed to come alive as though they were dancing and were transformed from disposable mass-produced products to precious unique forms,' he says. His lamps were used to create an installation at London's Design Museum in January 2004, and alongside Norcross's Eightfifty lampshade as part of the Victoria & Albert's 'Brilliant' exhibition. The forms of the lamps are beautiful, and the light shining through the Styrene has its own luminous quality. Cocksedge's other magical lights have included 'Watt', which involves connecting two points with a graphite pencil line to complete the circuit and make the light switch itself on, and 'Bulb', which uses the stem of a flower to conduct electricity through a vase of water.

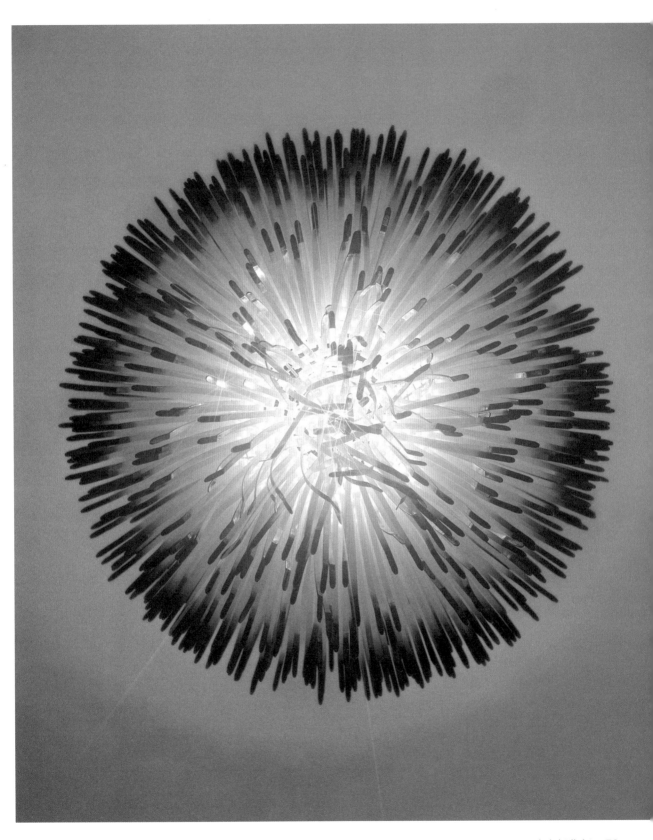

left Tejo Remy's 'Milk Bottle' chandelier for the innovative Dutch collective, Droog Design, is a fine example of using everyday objects to make something quite extraordinary.

right and far right Paul Cocksedge's Styrene lampshade is made by heating up polystyrene cups, giving a luminous honeycomb effect.

below right Georg Baldele's 1999 Buona Sera lampshade has a magical quality.

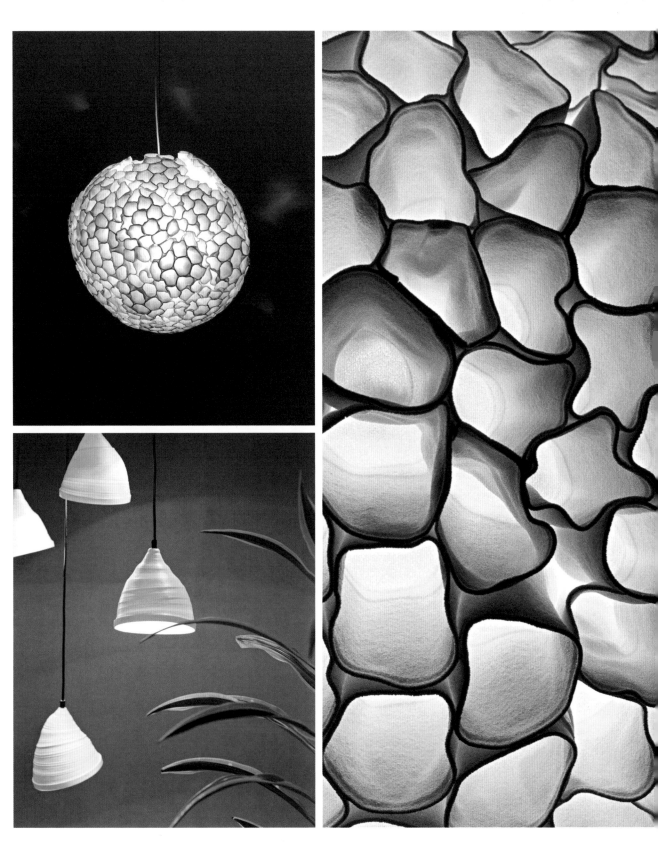

left Habitat's Boule Japonaise paper lantern has been in stock since the store opened in 1964. They are much loved by everyone, from students to architects.

right Paper can be draped, folded and threaded with wire to make a variety of styles of lampshade. It can be as simple or complicated as you like.

Paper lanterns are nothing new. The Boule Japonaise lampshade that Habitat first introduced in the 1960s has seemingly become almost as common as the light bulb itself. Wherever there's a bulb, it seems, there's a paper lampshade. There's something utterly charming about an uneven spiral of bamboo threading its way around the shade, the rough seams of rice paper, crudely glued together, and the complete, unpretentious simplicity of it all. But it doesn't take much to make this most humble of household essentials into something altogether more glamorous. Hanging several of them together at different heights creates a paper chandelier. And introducing a different shape and size, a splash of colour or even some pattern gives this old stalwart a new lease of life. Try hanging a really big lantern low over a dining table for a bit of 1970s atmosphere. Or use white shades with coloured bulbs inside dotted around the garden for a party with an oriental feel. Swaying in the breeze, and glowing in the dark, they will look truly magical.

tord boontje – from wednesday light to garland

Tord Boontje's Garland lampshade, designed for Habitat in 2002, is pure old-fashioned glamour. In gold or silver, its fragile flowers and foliage are a twenty-first-century baroque fairy tale. It is a lampshade and a work of art all in one. And it comes in the most basic form possible – a flat piece of acid-etched nickel-plated brass, packaged onto a stiff piece of corrugated cardboard. When wrapped around a light bulb, it is delicate and magical. Not surprisingly, it captured people's imaginations when it first appeared, not least because it was so affordable. The Garland grew from an original design by Boontje as part of his Wednesday project. The name refers to the most ordinary day in the middle of the week, and the designs within the project are all household items – a table, a chair, a lampshade. The Wednesday light is 1.5m (4½ft) of finely etched stainless steel draped around a light. Garland is a cheaper, more accessible version, like the ready-to-wear dress inspired by *haute couture*. 'Wednesday mixes the handmade and the machine made, the historical and the digital,' Boontje says. He uses modern technology to produce products inspired by decorative objects from the seventeenth and eighteenth centuries. Mass-production methods mean he can make magical, ethereal products at affordable prices.

Born in Enschede in the Netherlands in 1968, Boontje studied industrial design at Eindhoven Design Academy before going to the Royal College of Art in London. He graduated in 1994 and opened a workshop, working with recycled and ready-made materials. His Rough-and-Ready furniture is made from old pieces of wood and unwanted blankets. Instead of selling the chairs, he gives away plans and instructions for people to make their own, and he estimates that he has given away 30,000, although he cannot say how many have actually been made. He uses the chair – and a bench version – in his tiny south London studio. Boontje also collaborates on projects, including eyewear, with fashion designer Alexander McQueen, and has designed the ultimate in luxury – a chandelier called Blossom, using Swarovski crystals.

below left and right Boontje has extended his laser-cutting techniques to his Tyvek paper Midsummer lampshade, and he also works in Swarovski crystal for his Blossom chandelier.

right Tord Boontje's finely crafted Wednesday light has become the inspiration for the Garland, designed exclusively for Habitat and mass produced.

storage

There is a difference between creative clutter and chaotic clutter. Creative clutter is a form of self-expression. It is about showing off your interests and your personality. Some people collect shoes. Others collect plates, or toys, or vases, or typewriters. For some collectors, there is never enough space, and their collections take over their homes. The fashion designer Karl Lagerfeld famously had two houses next door to each other – one for him and one for his many collections. There is something much more interesting about a home that has some objects on display, and they don't have to be expensive or valuable in any way.

Anything displayed in quantity – whether it's key rings or rubber ducks – can look impressive and prevent a home looking sterile and soulless. It's all in the presentation. Arranging hooks on walls to create a hanging system is one solution. Glass display cabinets ensure that your collections don't get dusty. Bookshelves that stretch from floor to ceiling will always make your life's reading material look like a library, rather than a bookworm's fusty old hideaway. Shoes – especially if they are of the fabulous, high-heeled designer variety – can be stored and displayed at the same time in transparent boxes or simply on rows of shoe racks inside a cupboard so that you can see what you have and not always end up wearing the same pair. The odd pair of special shoes can look ultra-glamorous just left casually lying around. For some people, keeping their collections behind closed doors would be unimaginable.

They are as much part of everyday life as the sofa, bed or kitchen table. But there is a fine balance between having your possessions on display and your home beginning to look like a museum or gallery. It is important not to let your 'exhibits' take over (unless, of course, you want them to). Purpose-made display cases are an excellent way of keeping your objects contained. Look out for old store display units and bookcases in junk and vintage furniture stores. They will make your possessions – books, old tea sets, tin toys or stuffed animals – look instantly charming and keep them from getting dusty, too.

Most importantly, however, don't be overwhelmed by your possessions. Have regular clear-outs. You can always take a picture of a possession you no longer have room for, and put it in a frame on the wall, so it will still be on display.

right Why not display your favourite shoes on your staircase? High heels lead seductively upstairs. Make sure you only show off your best designer heels, not your worn-in trainers (sneakers) or your everyday flip-flops (thongs).

how to be organized

Despite computer technology, the paperless office – and home – has failed to happen for all but the most ruthlessly organized. Time-management experts advise that you should only touch each piece of paper once – to read it, file it or throw it away. But still, the paper builds up: tax returns, magazine cuttings, stationery, receipts, insurance documents, mortgage statements.

_ The key to being organized is to pick the right storage box for the right job – and label it accordingly.
_ For tax returns, separate your bills, invoices, stationery and statements into individual files as you go.

_ For photographs, keep your family albums up to date, and throw away the rejects.
_ Try to have a system – whether you file by size, by alphabet or by colour. If you are consistent, you will always know where everything is.
_ If all else fails, use clear Perspex boxes so that even if you don't label what's inside, at least you can see it at a glance.

far left Building some storage cupboards into a staircase is an ingenious solution for keeping things tidy in a small apartment.

left You can also build a chest of drawers under a child's bunk bed – just the thing for storing all those toy cars and Action Men.

right Sleek underbed storage is perfect for keeping bed linen and spare pillows handy for when guests stay.

concealing junk

If you don't want to display your belongings, storage is an essential part of your home. But minimal living takes a lot of time and discipline.

_ First of all, ask yourself if you need all these things. Have regular clear-outs. When was the last time you wore that dress, read that book or used that bag?

_ Take your cast-offs to your local charity store, or hold a garage sale.

_ Once you have reduced your excess baggage to a minimum, think carefully about how you store it. Built-in cupboards make the best use of space. Doors can be painted to match the walls so they become invisible.

_ Use boxes and drawers under your bed for clothes, bed linen and blankets.

_ Be inventive: hooks inside cupboard doors maximize hanging space.

_ Stow stuff inside boxes that double as stools, and look for cupboards, tables and side-boards that have plenty of storage space behind closed doors.

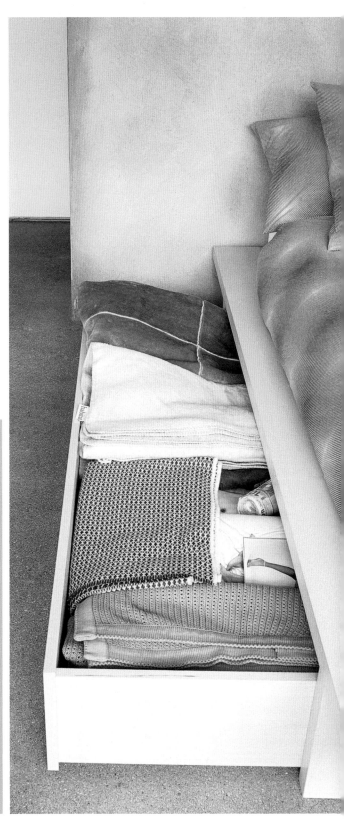

left Anna Castelli
Ferrieri's modular
storage can be used
in the bedroom, the
bathroom or stacked
up in the office.

below Frosted plastic
and Perspex can make
your clutter look cool
and minimal, but be
careful what you put
in see-through boxes.

boxing clever

Storage boxes come in whatever style and material suit
your lifestyle. Architect and designer Anna Castelli Ferrieri
designed the ultimate storage boxes in the 1960s. They are
stackable, interchangeable and modular – as flexible as
you want them to be. And with their retro styling, rounded
corners and space-age chic, they make storage something
altogether fabulous. Castelli Ferrieri started designing for
the Italian plastics company Kartell in 1966. But it is her
boxes that have been her lasting legacy to an increasingly
acquisitive generation. We use them all around the house,
from the bedroom, where they make the perfect bedside
table, with enough room to store books and magazines, to
the bathroom, where they are just the thing for hiding away
toilet paper, nappies (diapers) and any other clutter.

If you want something a little more down to earth and
functional, you will find what you are looking for with good
old-fashioned archive boxes. Habitat's Cargo boxes, made
from recycled cardboard with metal reinforced corners, are
storage classics. They were originally British navy standard
issue and have been a staple at Habitat since the 1970s.
Invaluable for organizing everything from paperwork to
CDs, magazine cuttings and photographs, they have such
a utility look about them, you'll hardly notice they are there.

love 6

create 10

indulge 20

dress your home

share 116

imagine 168

Dressing your home is a little like dressing yourself. You have particular colours that you think suit you, regardless of whether they are in or out of fashion. And you have other colours – say, lime green, or orange with purple polka dots – that you wear simply because they are 'in' that season and the shops are full of them.

They might not suit you, but you are seduced by what's in vogue, and it makes a change from your usual palette of black or beige. The walls and textiles of your home are not very different. We tend to stick to certain neutrals and then inject the odd bit of colour – or even a spot of print in the form of a wallpaper or a cushion cover – to keep up with fashion. Of course, most of us don't change the colour of our walls as quickly as we change the colour of our socks or scarves. But in an ideal world, we might have a single wall that we repaint every so often, according to our mood, or even to reflect the change in the seasons outside. It wouldn't be such a big decision as painting an entire room. If we got it wrong once in a while, we could just paint over it again. And it would be the surest way of injecting a fresh perspective and new life into our homes.

Despite the fact that most of us decide on a colour for our walls and then don't change it until we move house, colour, and how we use it, is all about fashion. Think of the 1960s, and it's all silver and white and space age. Or it's a riot of shiny apple greens, purples and oranges, courtesy of Verner Panton. This Danish designer, whose futuristic designs would have looked at home in a UFO or on a *Star Trek* planet far, far away in the solar system, experimented with colour as much as he did with materials and shape. His parallel colour experiments combined colours that were close to each other in the colour spectrum – so close that they vibrated when placed next to each other.

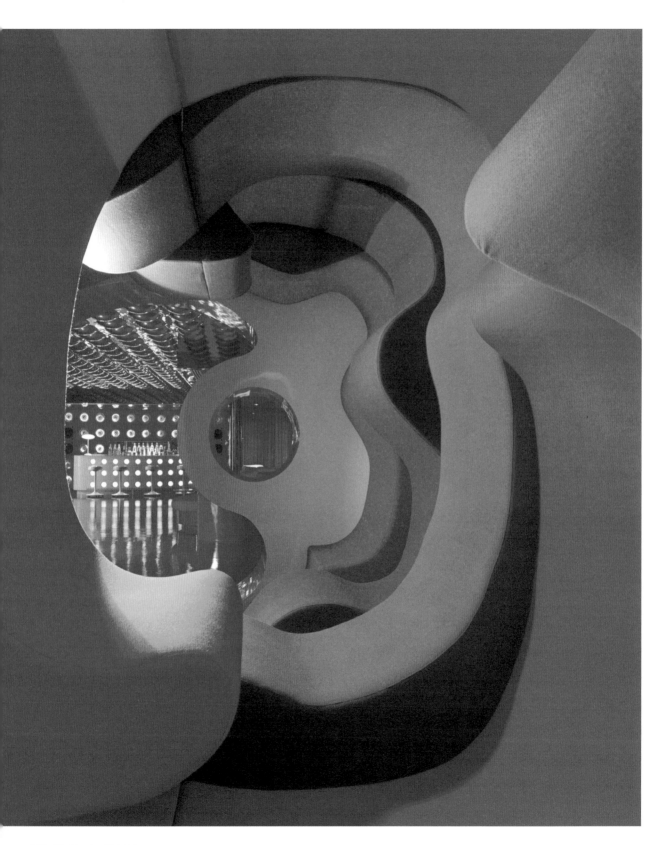

'When working on a prototype, I usually start with a white version so as not to let the colour distract me,' Panton said in 1986, in an interview to celebrate his sixtieth birthday. 'But the ideal, of course, is for both colour and form to harmonize. For me, colour plays a greater role than form.' So when designing the interior of a restaurant, such as the Astoria in Trondheim in 1960, everything would be bathed in shades of red, from the geometric patterned carpets to the matching walls, the tables and chairs and, of course, the lights. If you happened to be wearing red, you would all but disappear. Or else he would make walls and ceilings that glowed with luminous coloured light. On board the ship *Visiona II*, the interior of which he designed in 1970, these experiments in colour could be seen at their most extreme. He created dream-like landscapes in Dralon that looked like some trippy vision of the surface of the moon, with intense shades of blue blurring into shocking pink and warm, womb-like red. If that was all too much for you, you could simply have one of his rugs, with their concentric circles of blues and reds, like an art student's study of the colour wheel. In fact, Panton reinvented the colour wheel with his own 'colour line', which had as a starting point three yellows, three reds, three blues and three greens. For him, bare white rooms were just a waste of space.

When the singer Lenny Kravitz bought a 1950s ranch house in Miami, he commissioned his friend the interior designer Michael Czysz of Architropolis to convert it from the rich Jewish bachelor pad it was to something a little more out of this world. Bearing in mind Kravitz's own musical leanings towards the 1960s and 1970s, Czysz turned the house into a psychedelic homage to Verner Panton, re-creating the luminous colour walls, the clashes of orange and red (said to stimulate the appetite), the geometric patterns and shapes, and even the shag-pile carpet. Panton, who died in 1998, would have been proud. Over 30 years on, his colourful work is as inspiring and influential as it ever was. In a way, the rest of the world has never quite caught up with his unique vision.

But trends come and go. In the 1970s there was a craze for avocado-green bathrooms (just as there was for the fruit itself); dark cork tiles; orange plastic; thick shag-pile carpets; purple and pink walls; chocolate brown and mustard. Texture was in – be it hairy and shaggy carpets and cushions, or rough crazy paving or slate fireplaces. Even walls were given the treatment, with craggy Artex plastering that threatened to take a layer of skin off if you brushed against it. In the 1980s things were much sleeker, smoother and shinier. Walls were white, or papered with red and white checks. Floors were stripped. The colour palette was severe – black, white and primary red; grey if you were arty. There were lots of reflective surfaces – mirror, glass and chrome. Less was definitely more. Then, in the 1990s, our homes became a bit more free and easy. We painted our walls sunshine shades of yellow

left Verner Panton's psychedelic colour scapes added an intensity and depth to his interiors. The colour surrounds you.

overleaf There are many ways to dress your home. Try personalized wallpaper made from favourite magazine cuttings and photographs pasted directly onto the wall to make a collage.

'I love to design clothes; I love to design homes. I know the way I like a silhouette to look on my body, and I know the way I like to live. Fashion and design, it's all the same, man.'
Lenny Kravitz, singer

and orange, as well as neutral shades of cream and white. We liked blond wood, and aspired to loft living, with bare brick walls, industrial pillars and wood beams. Our kitchens were stainless steel, from the appliances to the splashback. Our floors were still wood, but we liked to tile our kitchen floors, and our bathrooms, too. Pattern became more fashionable towards the end of the decade, with retro geometric wallpapers, stripy rugs and spotty Damien Hirst bed linen finding their way into our homes.

As for the twenty-first century, well so far it has been all about mixing and matching, being eclectic, being individual and showing off your personality through your home. We like to experiment with a colour block – maybe bitter chocolate, or dark khaki green – on a single wall. We sometimes have carpet rather than hard flooring because it's comfortable underfoot. If we're being ironic, we might even lay a bit of shag pile in a living room or a bedroom. We like hairy cushions and rough throws. We might tile our bathrooms in cork once more. Our homes have become more sensory, tactile experiences. We like to mix and match our sofas and chairs with pattern and colour. We mix wood, leather and wool. We add a piece of brightly coloured Perspex – a coffee table, say, or a lampshade. If anything, things have come full circle to the ideas of Verner Panton – although few dare to be quite so extreme.

For most of us, colour, pattern and texture – and knowing what to do with them – can be quite scary. But they are the basics of the home, the backdrop for everything else. It's very easy to simply choose white, and stick with it. Certainly, for some minimalists, white is the only choice. It's clean, it's neutral – a blank canvas. But for others, white is simply a get-out clause, an easy way not to have to make difficult decisions. In the natural world, there is no rhyme or reason to the way colour and texture clash joyfully together: the bright reds and greens of a poppy field; the hard yellow of sunflowers; the endless shades of grey in a heavy sky. Everywhere you look, colour, texture and pattern are working hard together, jarring, blending and upstaging each other. If you follow nature, you can't go far wrong, whether you are looking at the metallic greys, duck-egg blues and emerald greens displayed on a shingle beach washed by the sea, or the wild clashes of acid-bright colour, hard grasses and feathery birds of a tropical jungle.

Think of your home as if it were a garden – the texture and colour are the hard landscaping, while pattern is the planting. If you like an English country garden, then your home should be alive with blousy blooms and soft, juicy colours. If you prefer a bit of decking and shingle, some concrete stools and a few architectural grasses, then so, too, should your home be harder and more industrial. Whatever your preference, there are no restrictions or rules. You simply match your colours, and shop around until your home is dressed just the way you want it.

colour

right Primary colours can be used to make a home look bold and modern. For a stylish effect, think Mondrian rather than pre-school.

Colour cards can be very confusing. There you are, simply wanting to paint your living room cream. But it's not so easy; there are 20 different shades. There's off-white. Bone. Magnolia. Clotted cream. So how do you choose the right one? Of course, there are tester pots, so you can try them out on your own walls. But even then, it is difficult to make a decision. And cream is a neutral shade. When it comes to choosing bolder colours for your home, you have to have confidence and vision. It might be a matter of falling in love with a particular colour – such as Tiffany blue, or the red of a Coca-Cola can. Then, all you have to do is take a swatch to a friendly paint mixer to have it matched.

When deciding on colour schemes, it helps to create your own mood board, with fabric and colour swatches, wallpapers, inspirations and ideas. Simply treat it as a scrapbook or a pin board, and add all of the elements until you have a complete picture. Understanding the colour wheel helps. It's very simple. There are three primary colours – blue, red and yellow – and every other colour is a combination of these. The primaries are separated by the colours they make when combined – the secondary colours. So blue and red will have purple in between; red and yellow will be separated by orange. The variations are endless. Your colour wheel can be as big as you want it to be. The basic rule is that colours opposite each other are complementary, say, blue and orange. Use one colour as the dominant shade, with the other to highlight it. You can also combine colours within the same third of the wheel, or colours spaced evenly a third of the wheel apart. Of course, you can ignore all of this advice and simply go on instinct and what makes you feel good to look at.

Colour is an emotional business. Young babies are supposed to like soft shades of pink because it reminds them of their time in the comfort of their mother's womb. Right from the beginning, we are surrounded by colour. And according to colour therapists, what we choose can affect our mood and how we feel when we are in different parts of our homes. Indigo, for example, is seen as a sedative, associated with divine knowledge and the higher mind – a good choice then for the bedroom or study. Green is a balancing and harmonizing colour that can be used anywhere. If used on its own, however, the result might be total inertia and indecision. Yellow, in contrast, stimulates mental activity and makes you feel more confident, so is a good choice for entrance halls and living rooms. Orange warms and energizes. It is the colour of fun and makes us sociable – good for kitchens, living rooms and playrooms. Red energizes the emotions and stimulates the appetite, which is helpful in a dining room, though a dark red can make a small space feel claustrophobic. For a calm mood choose turquoise; perfect for bathrooms to soothe our immune and nervous systems and make us feel as though we are in the sea. White emphasizes purity and promotes clarity. But it can be too cold and needs to be broken up.

colours of the world

Every country has a different colour story to tell. And depending on where you are, and what the light is like, colours take on their own personality. A sienna yellow in Italy might look completely different if taken out of its context. Sometimes colours – like the local culinary specialities – just don't travel. Whitewashed houses with red geraniums in the window boxes look dazzling in the Mediterranean sun, but lose their sparkle under murky northern European skies. Nevertheless, we are continually inspired by our travels, and our homes are all the more interesting for it. It's not just about what we put on our walls. We can inject colour by simply adding a jade green vase, or a splash of warmth in the form of a lamp, a throw, a rug or a cushion. So a pair of bowls in turquoise and orange, bought from a Moroccan souk, will bring its own little ray of sunshine into a corner of your home. Or you might love the bowls so much that they become the inspiration for an entire colour scheme, from your curtains to your rugs. The secret is to keep your eyes open, and take photos, swatches, souvenirs and mental notes wherever you go. Your home will be all the richer for it.

'Colour is very difficult. You either have an eye for it, or you don't. Follow your instinct – you're invariably right first time. Women usually have a good feeling for colour. I advise people to just try things out. I always show clients my sister Neisha's wallpaper collection – not just because she's my sister, but because they really are the most beautiful papers. Why not experiment? Wallpaper a stairwell or a wall in the living room. You can always paint over it.'

Charlotte Crosland, interior decorator

left Indian pinks and reds add an exotic richness to a room.

right Cool blue walls mixed with decorative tiles are pure Morocco. This room will remain cool even in the height of summer.

global inspirations

We tend to associate different colours with particular countries around the world:

_ India is perhaps the most vividly colourful place, with its turmeric yellows, madder pinks and bright crimson reds.
_ Morocco has its spicy colours of saffron, henna and ginger; the Tuareg, the nomads of the desert, whose skin used to be dyed as deeply blue as their clothes; and the Majorelle Gardens in Marrakesh, with their distinctive shade of almost electric blue.
_ New Zealand has its lush landscape of verdant greens.
_ Cuba's sun-faded palette epitomizes 1950s cool.

_ Spain has its blindingly white villages, especially in the south.
_ Africa's savannah grasslands suggest dry, earthy tones.
_ Japan, with its Tokyo neon, is unremittingly monochrome.
_ Ireland has its ever-changing palette of leaden grey skies.
_ China, whatever the ruling political system, is forever associated with red – whether it be Imperial red or the communist flag.

neutrals with an accent

Most of us opt for neutral tones of pale creams, beiges and off-whites that blend into one another without too much effort. There is a reason for this: they stand the test of time, and by using them you avoid your home looking too bright or garish. Tasteful neutrals are the best choice if you plan to sell your home in the near future as they don't offend. They allow a space to breathe. However, too much 'greige' can become a little bland. The best way to use classic neutrals is as a backdrop, with the occasional splash of colour to break up the monotones. You might paint a single strip of colour along a wall. Or add jewel-coloured door handles. Or simply include a collection of vases in shades of vivid reds, dark aubergines or bright blues to give a room an injection of energy. Soft furnishings such as rugs and cushions can freshen up a room, making it look up to date even if the rest of it stays the same.

below A blue chair gives a light, neutral room a modern twist, while a hint of black adds focus to a white room.

right A classic white room is given warmth with splashes of hot red and orange. Colour can be in the accessories. You don't have to commit with paint.

love your home

Heti Gervis, colour consultant,
red throw from Habitat
'One of the most enjoyable things
about my home is colour – on the
walls and in all the bits and pieces
I have accumulated. I love the colour
in my living room. I have used a
casein paint, which has a chalky
quality that seems to change colour
during the course of the day. I often
move rooms around depending on
my mood and get an instant colour
fix by adding throws and cushions.'

warm and cosy colours

Shades of red, pink, orange and yellow can fill a room
with light and warmth, even where there is none. Think
cocoon, think womb, and you will be well on your way
to creating a cosy nest. The secret of using a palette of
warm colours is to choose the right shades. Go for darker
tones – a dark red rather than a bright one, a dusky orange
rather than a vivid one, and yellow ochre rather than pale
lemon – and you will create a room with more atmosphere
than your favourite smoky bar. Aubergine has become one
of the most fashionable colours of the new millennium – a
much more subtle and sophisticated shade than the purple
favoured in the 1970s. Bitter chocolate and rich berry
colours – blackcurrant, raspberry and loganberry – are all
shades that will add warmth without making you feel as
though you are living in a kaleidoscope. Keeping your paint
matt also makes a room look rich and velvety.

below left Aubergine
bed linen merges
perfectly with dark
wooden panelling.

below right Blues and
greys are rendered
warm and welcoming
with a modern hearth.

right Add texture and
colour with cushions –
and don't be afraid to
inject a hit of orange.

left Yellow, white and black make a strong contrasting colour scheme. Even the flowers coordinate.

below left Shades of blue give a room a bright and breezy, summery feel. If you introduce colour on a sofa, there is no need to paint the walls any shade other than white.

below right Sombre greys and soft lights have a calming effect in the bedroom.

cool colours – light and shade

The kind of daylight (if any) in a room affects the way colours work within it. If you have a room with lots of natural light and sunshine throughout the day, any colour you choose will always look its best, although remember that bright colours will look even brighter. So if you don't want to have to wear sunglasses, maybe tone it down a little. And avoid brilliant white. Rooms without a lot of natural light can look a little chilly (especially in the winter), so avoid blues and greys and opt for something a little rosier. Rooms that face east or west have varying light throughout the day. If you use an east-facing room in the morning, the light will be warm. But if your favourite breakfast spot faces west, then you may need to paint the room with something a little warm and sunny to compensate. You can be clever and combine cold and warm colours – blues and oranges, say – to reflect the changing light pattern throughout the day.

shocking clashes – that work!

Anything goes – well, almost. If you have the confidence and the nerve, you can experiment and play with colour to make unusual combinations that make a room look creative and alive with personality. Play with your colour wheel and concentrate on the secondary colours – violet and green, orange and purple, pink and aquamarine. If it sets your teeth on edge just thinking about it, then don't do it. But if you crave excitement in a room, this is the surest way of getting it. Of course, there is no point combining colours that simply make you feel seasick. Go for subtle vibrations rather than total dizziness. And don't mix up too many colours in one room. A pure fuchsia pink will positively glow if you add a hint of milky jade. A crazy acid-coloured deck chair-striped fabric will look super-cool on a sofa set against a backdrop of burnt orange. And a green wall with a flash of red – a picture frame, say, or simply a vase of flowers – will look seriously exotic.

below Strong colours work well together in hard blocks. Shiny red chairs and a monolithic table look even sharper against a backdrop of acid yellow.

right Fuchsia pink and red make for a spicy combination, cooled down with the addition of duck-egg blue walls. Pink, red and magenta clash gloriously, making the room almost vibrate.

'Wearing colour says so much about your state of mind. In your home, colour is a more private affair. It's your intimate space – you choose who comes to your home. Nowadays, colour is everywhere, from computers to phones. We are becoming braver with colour and how we use it. I use my home as a laboratory for my work. It is like a mood board, reflecting my collections each season.'

Matthew Williamson, fashion designer

pattern

right Pattern can be subtle, as well as bold and bright, or pretty and girly. This tablecloth is a witty, modern take on old-fashioned lace.

Pattern is easy to introduce into your home, and it can make such a difference. It adds personality and warmth. Inspiration for pattern comes from everywhere. As well as the classic stripes and checks that will always be around, the surface decoration in our homes – from our walls to our teapots – can be referenced from anywhere and anything. The types of pattern we choose say a lot about who we are. The recent resurgence in interest in wallpapers has opened up a whole new world. Do we choose something familiar and traditional? Something wild and kitsch? Something that suits the period of our home? Or something new and contemporary? And while most of us still shy away from covering our entire homes with surface decoration, many of us opt for a single wall, a hallway, or even just a section of wallpaper in a frame.

Living with print can be difficult. You have to be really in love with something before you can comfortably paste it all over your walls – unless, of course, it is something so neutral you barely notice it. If the sheer expanse of wallpaper scares you, it might simply be a matter of adding a decorated cushion here and a vase there. Lampshades can be a good way to introduce some pattern. They are inexpensive and can be updated every season – or when you get bored. Cover books with favourite wrapping papers. You might even have a treasured silk kimono with a pattern you love. Hang it on the wall and you will enjoy it far more than if it is stashed away in a wardrobe.

Wallpaper doesn't have to come ready-printed on a roll. It's something you can create yourself, either by having your favourite snaps blown up larger than life to make your own photographic art, or by pasting a wall with a collage of your favourite pictures, postcards or magazine cuttings. More dramatically, *trompe-l'oeil* paint effects can transform a wall into a lush landscape or urban cityscape. Look out for old patterned china vases or cups and saucers, and display them together on a mantelpiece or on a shelf. Likewise, a few odd tiles propped up against a wall can make an interesting backdrop. It's all about individual taste and whatever catches your eye. Your personal collections can become your wallpaper, too.

left Cole & Son's Flamingo wallpaper is quirky and fun, but charming, too. Used on a single wall, it will create dramatic impact and make a room unforgettable.

right This bestselling 'Asuka' cabbage flower print is by Osborne & Little. The oversized florals add more than a touch of chintz, but the Eastern-style pattern retains a simplicity. This striking gold colourway would be perfect for a dining area.

right centre This vintage botanical wallpaper by Florence Broadhurst will bring a bit of the natural countryside into the home. It is perfect for the bedroom or a living-room wall.

far right Neisha Crosland's geometric prints have a timeless appeal – a good choice for hallways and stairs.

geometric

Spots, stripes and checks form the backbone of any collection of wallpapers or fabrics. But they needn't be traditional. Geometric patterns can play tricks with your eyes. The Bridget Riley Op Art stripe has been given a new lease of life by fashion designers including Paul Smith and textile companies such as Kvadrat. These Danish fabric specialists were responsible for producing Verner Panton's Optic prints in the 1960s as well as Arne Jacobsen's geometric patterns, which still look as modern as ever.

When textile designer Niki Jones joined Habitat in 1999, one of the first things she did was to update a classic madras check. 'Then, computers were a relatively recent introduction to design studios,' she remembers. 'And the way you could pixelate an image was interesting.' The result was a design with an unusually high number of colours – nine in the warp and nine in the weft, which gives it an almost three-dimensional quality. It looks as though ribbons of colour are woven through each other. It is a modern, high-tech fabric that has become a classic.

Be creative in the way you use geometrics. Play with scale. Match big spots with thin stripes, and don't restrict yourself to the walls. Spots look great on the floor, while checks and stripes can update a sofa or a single wall.

making a graphic statement

_ Paint vertical stripes of varying thicknesses in five or six contrasting colours on one wall. Use a spirit level to draw your guide lines then use masking tape when you are painting – make sure you allow each colour to dry before moving on to the next one. This is a great technique for a nursery – done in primary colours, it will provide a visually stimulating environment for a baby without being overly cute, as many nursery schemes can be.
_ Frame a favourite piece of wallpaper to use geometric pattern on a small scale. Or create an optical illusion by overlaying a simple black-and-white striped wallpaper with a series of framed square sections of the same paper – position the frames so that the black stripes line up with the white ones. Keep the frames as simple as possible, or use clip frames with no surround, so that they do not detract from the effect.
_ Use fabric or paper in a boldly spotted or checked pattern to cover your photo albums or filing boxes. Align them on a shelf or place a few on a coffee table for a readily interchangeable boost of pattern.

far left Verner Panton's geometric black and white rug becomes the focal point of a living room.

left Stripy bed linen in juicy colours is a more relaxed version of a traditional stripe.

right Broad egg shapes outlined on a pale blue background make a soft graphic statement.

café tablecloth

A red and white gingham tablecloth is visual shorthand for a cosy kitchen supper. All that's missing is the Aga, a cat curled up in front of the fire and a plate of something simple, warm and comforting such as macaroni cheese. Gingham is the most homely of fabrics. It's like a dose of Doris Day – old-fashioned, wholesome and fabulously 1950s. There is something very clean, simple and fresh about it. A gingham tablecloth is a bistro staple, but it is as at home in a domestic setting as a black and white tiled kitchen floor or a Welsh dresser packed with china. It looks right on any table, from the rural country house to the inner-city apartment – or laid out on the sand at a seaside picnic. Although red and white is the classic colourway, it also works in yellow, green, lilac, blue or pink. The basic check is a universal language. But it needn't be confined to the table. For a vintage look, use gingham to cover open-fronted kitchen cupboard units – simply thread the fabric onto a length of curtain wire and hook it onto each side of the frame. Or make it into simple curtains for your kitchen windows for that 1950s feel. And if you want to continue with the Doris Day theme, make it into an apron and bake an apple pie.

In a world that is less than secure, there is something very comforting about vintage patterns and designs. It's the familiarity of seeing something your grandparents might have had or that you have seen in books or museums. Whether it's an art deco motif from the 1930s, a space-age sputnik abstract from the 1950s or a naive colourscape from the 1970s, we can't resist looking to the past when decorating our homes. Often, new designs are inspired by the old. There might simply be a passing resemblance, or it might be a full-blown reproduction. Different periods enjoy different moments in the sun. The 1970s – in particular the childlike designs from Finnish company Marimekko – have been enjoying a recent resurgence. In turn, they have inspired a new generation of designers who are seeing them for the first time. Habitat diehards may remember buying them first time round.

Lucienne Day

The British textile designer Lucienne Day has become a strong influence again. Her work from the 1950s has a period look about it, but she was also resolutely modern in her approach. Her designs had a similar feel to some of the textiles being produced at the time by Charles and Ray Eames in the United States. Her classic design Calyx, made for the Festival of Britain in 1951, was a defining moment in twentieth-century design. Inspired by the paintings of Miró and Kandinsky, the result was totally modern and innovative. Her work was both painterly and abstract. Florals were never romantic, but might simply be represented by a spare line drawing. Her designs were always graphic and used a unique palette of colours. As well as producing prints for fabrics for the London furniture and interiors store Heal's, she also applied her minimal eye to ceramics and tableware for Rosenthal. Along with her husband, Robin Day, Lucienne was commemorated as a Twentieth-Century Legend by Habitat in 1999 (see page 38).

far left Lucienne Day's Calyx print has become an icon of the 1950s.

left A 1960s geometric print in shades of yellow and orange still looks contemporary today.

right Try to resist the temptation to strip off original wallpapers from your home. A single wall of vintage floral will add character, and you will keep part of your home's history.

left Florals and checks make great bedfellows. Don't worry if your bed linen doesn't match – it's more fun that way. Add a differently patterned throw over the top for a romantic country cottage look.

below right Paisley is a traditional print and looks great on a fluffy eiderdown. Look out for vintage quilts in junk shops. They often have more character than new ones.

english eccentric

The English country garden is an enduring influence on textile designers and home decorators, keen to bring the outdoors in. Big chintzy blooms – chrysanthemums, lupins, bluebells, daisies and roses – add romance, comfort and a general feeling of wellbeing to the home. Florals go in and out of fashion. If you are going to use them, you have to revel in their colour and richness. Don't use anything too twee or insipid. Big, oriental patterns are preferable to polite, little spriggy flowers. The Australian designer Florence Broadhurst had the right idea with her extraordinary theatrical wallpapers of the 1960s and 1970s. Not surprisingly, the kitschest and campest oriental blooms from her archives are enjoying a revival, and can be seen gracing the walls of New York's Soho House and the chicest of boutique hotels in Brighton.

The other traditional patterns that have gained new credibility are paisley and flock. There is a certain irony in the use of flock – until recently seen only on the walls of Indian restaurants. The original inspiration for this 1970s nightmare was the real thing – the extremely luxurious wool flocked paper that was used to embellish the grandest of establishments, including the walls of the English gentlemen's clubs of India in the 1930s. It is still made by the north London wallpaper specialists Cole & Son. The company has been going strong since 1875, and the contemporary collection includes a fabulous pink and red paisley, Rajapur; some amazing flamingos on gold; and its recent award winner, Hummingbird. A house full of florals and chintzes – not to mention the odd flamingo – is the mark of a true English eccentric.

left Striped wallpaper, coloured mosaic and a mixture of colours and textures give a kitchen energy and vibrancy. Paint the insides of shelves and storage units in colours to match, and look out for brightly coloured bowls and kitchen utensils.

below Crocheted, patchwork and floral blankets can make a room look homey and lived-in. The more different patterns and textures, the merrier.

mixing and matching

Rules are made to be broken. Just as there is a move towards a more hand-crafted approach in furniture and design, there is also a move away from the home looking fully coordinated and matching. By picking out interesting pieces of pattern – whether for a wall, a cushion, a tea cup or the bed linen – and mixing them together, we are making our homes more individual and less off-the-shelf. It's a magpie approach that gives us the freedom to mix old and new, good taste and bad taste, kitsch and serious. Of course, there is an art to avoiding your home looking like a jumble (rummage) sale. You need to maintain a careful eye to ensure your decorative treasures look like heirlooms and not junk. Be careful what you buy. Try to restrict yourself to things you really love. And don't worry if there are a few clashes of pattern along the way. That's half the fun.

dos and don'ts

_ Don't be afraid of breaking the rules. Mix checked and striped, spotted and plain fabrics together. There is no right or wrong.
_ Do be aware of how colours work together. Keep to similar shades and your patterns should work well.
_ Don't forget scale. Mix big polka dots with little ones, fat stripes with fine pinstripes.
_ Do use plain colours to break up areas where the pattern is too busy.
_ Do paint your own patterns on a wall. Copy designs you like from wallpaper, wrapping paper or even decorative book endpapers.

texture

right Use unexpected textures in unusual places. Green baize was used to cover the kitchen units in this raw, industrial-look loft. The shiny resin floor accentuates the matt cupboard doors.

Our homes would be very boring places without any differences in texture – a hardwood floor, a thick shaggy rug, a shiny glass table. It is the rough and the smooth, the shiny and the matt that are as important to the way a home feels as the colours on the walls and the smell of coffee in the morning. Often the way we experience the textures within our homes is unconscious. But the smoothness of a wooden banister rail or the shininess of a cupboard door can be what attracts us to buy them in the first place.

Floors can really change the way a home looks and feels. The trend away from carpets to wooden floors has shifted again, back to carpets. These might not be wall to wall and fitted to every nook and cranny, but a shag-pile rug will certainly add another dimension to a room. In bathrooms, there are many alternatives, too, from rubber, which is warm and comforting underfoot, to cork, slate, limestone or good old-fashioned ceramic tile. For kitchens, anything goes, from natural Marmoleum to the classic terracotta. And once you've decided on the floor, simply build layer upon layer of texture on top.

In the 1960s and 1970s, when shag-pile carpets were all the rage, synthetic fibres were all part of the modern home. A few sparks of static electricity were commonplace. Artificial fibres were part of a revolution that helped make our homes easier to maintain and manage. Add a touch of polyester to your cotton sheets and the creases drop out as they dry – no need for hours of ironing. Synthetics could mimic the look of natural fibres while making them cheaper, washable, stretchable and more accessible. And plastic replaced wood and metal for making almost anything. These days, the tendency is to treat synthetics with suspicion and go for real wood and 100 per cent cotton, wool or silk wherever possible. But scratch the surface and you will find that man-made materials have simply become increasingly smart. A taffeta curtain might look and act like silk, but is actually made of viscose or acetate. And as long as it does the job, we don't particularly care. A bath towel might have a touch of synthetic in it, but it simply makes the towel softer and fluffier, so that's fine too. And plastic is now so sophisticated it has become a luxury material in its own right, valued just as much as oak or stainless steel.

rough and ready

Industrial spaces – factories, artists' studios, restaurants and warehouses – have had a great influence on the domestic interior in recent decades. We peel off plaster to reveal the bare brick underneath; we pour concrete floors and treat them as a feature rather than a foundation to be covered by something else; and we use brushed steel everywhere, from electrical fittings to kitchen units. It is no longer necessary for our homes to be 'finished'. It's either urban industrial or country rustic, with untreated wood, painted brick and stone floors. Either way, the look is rugged, rough and ready.

Perhaps one of the most surprising industrial materials to find inside the home is concrete. But the material has been given a new lease of life, not just in the form of worktops and floors, but in furniture and accessory design, too. Slabs of it are used as tea-light holders – the perfect combination of the delicate and the brutal – as well as for bathtubs (the ultimate luxury, but make sure you fill it first if you want to avoid a chill), fireplaces and chairs.

Materials in their natural state make interesting surfaces within the home. Look out for all things hairy, scratchy and crunchy – the sort of things you might find while out on a country ramble. Hessian (burlap), seagrass, wicker, calico, denim, rubber, banana leaf, rattan and cardboard all add a new dimension to your living space. Perhaps the easiest natural material to live with is wood. But look out for interesting knots and organic shapes. From a practical point of view, the rougher and tougher a surface, the more wear and tear it will be able to take. These are not materials to treat preciously.

below left Industrial materials can work well within the domestic environment. Cork tiles give this kitchen a well-worn rustic look. They are also very practical and ecologically sound.

right Bare metal and brick walls give an industrial edge. This is a room that will take a lot of wear and tear. It is entirely functional. Even the chipped paint and bare metal on the bed frame are left in their raw state.

feel your way

_ Opposites attract. Mix the rough with the smooth, the matt with the shiny and the hard with the soft.
_ Shiny materials such as plastic, glass and mirror reflect light and make a room glamorous. But make sure you keep the surfaces clean. Use the appropriate polish to avoid smears.
_ Look for long-tufted rugs to give your home a raw edge.
_ Go by instinct. Choose fabrics because of how they feel, as well as how they look.
_ Mix up your paint finishes. Matt walls can look like velvet, while glossy walls will add extra shine.

trends in trees

There are fashions in wood as with everything else. Over the past few years, designers have been using a lot of light oak. It looks solid and modern and honest. The Victorians loved a bit of dark mahogany, while for homeowners of the 1970s, pine was all the rage. In the 1990s, the wood to be seen with was deepest, darkest wenge. Now there is a move back towards darker, more exotic hardwoods such as rosewood and walnut, guaranteed to make any piece of furniture look exotic, and very, very expensive. For the modernist, however, the wood of choice will always be plywood. People are obsessed with the material, made by glueing together layers of veneer-thin birch or beech. It's the designer's choice of wood and has been made into seminal pieces of furniture by everyone from Alvar Aalto to Charles and Ray Eames to Robin Day.

left The type of cladding more usually seen on garden sheds gives this bedroom a woody, treehouse feel.

above Plywood is a universally cheap and flexible material with cult appeal.

left A squashy sofa is given extra comfort with big, fat cushions. Living rooms should be places for relaxing, entertaining and socializing. If you want to be a couch potato, this is just the place to do it.

right Shaggy mohair and sheepskin make for a furry combination. All you need is a fluffy dog, and the domestic picture is complete.

how to wash a sheepskin rug

1 Pre-soak your rug in lukewarm water with a mild wool detergent, then give it a gentle hand-wash. The bathtub might be the best place.
2 Rinse until the water is clear.
3 Comb the pile while still damp – you can use a soft hairbrush.
4 Slow drying is best. Hang away from the sun's rays or from direct heat sources to avoid the rug drying out too quickly.
5 When almost dry, stretch the rug by hand in all directions, and finally stretch it into shape.
6 Once dry, fluff the pile up again with your hairbrush.

soft and cosy

Every nest needs some feathers to make it warm and welcoming, whether it is a big squashy sofa, some plump, soft cushions for the floor, or the fluffiest of sheepskin rugs. These are the textures that seduce us into buying them, and seduce us into staying in at night – even if there is a party to go to or a new film to see. These are the things that make a home luxurious and inviting.

In the bedroom, there are endless opportunities for creating a comfort zone. You might prefer carpet here so that it is soft and warm underfoot. For the bed itself there are throws – satin quilts, velvet blankets, fake fur rugs – and stacks of pillows, the bigger and fatter the better. A bed should make you want to sink into it and never get up again. And there is more romance – if that is what you want from a bedroom – in curtains rather than blinds.

It's a seriously sensory experience. Touch a butter-soft cashmere cushion cover, and you are smitten. You won't want your sofa to wear anything else. Or feel the long tufts of lambswool carpet between your toes and you'll want to walk barefoot – around the house, at least – for ever. Our homes can be as luxurious as we want them to be simply by choosing the materials that give us that feelgood factor.

love your home

Rachel Loos, *writer and former editor of* Elle Decoration, *Dart rug from Habitat* 'It's about being in a place that is totally yours – it's comfortable and makes you feel happy; it's lovely to be surrounded by things you are passionate about. Your home is your haven, where you can do whatever you want to.'

hard and shiny

Rooms need shiny surfaces. They set off other textures, reflecting them along with any light caught along the way. And they give us something to polish. Glass and Perspex are sure to add glamour to any environment because of the way they shine. There is something altogether more masculine, however, about metals. Chrome was the big favourite in the 1980s – as well as in the 1930s, when it was used to great effect alongside mirrors. But metals have now become so commonplace in the home, from our aluminium trashcans to our stainless-steel cutlery and our wire shelving systems, that they are not so much of a statement anymore. Metals now form part of the structure of our homes. There are, however, times when it can still stand out. It might be an industrial-steel lampshade, or a Bauhaus chair made out of tubular steel. Just because a metal isn't precious, it doesn't mean it can't be the star of the show. And as well as the everyday metals we are all used to, there are some rising stars – including titanium, useful because it is so light – and an old industrial material with a new domestic application, which is as heavy and monumental as they come – cast iron.

left Habitat's clear Perspex table is hard and shiny, and strangely invisible. Its ingenious design allows you to see all the workings and construction details.

right Stainless-steel mirror balls surround this futuristic swimming pool, and reflect both the sky above and the water's surface below.

caring for shiny surfaces

Stainless steel can mark very easily. All it takes is a few fingerprints or a watermark and it can look a mess. But the solution is quick and easy. All you need is a bottle of baby oil or olive oil and some cotton wool. Wipe the offending marks with a tiny dab of oil – they will disappear as if by magic. Glass can also be a high-maintenance surface. A good glass-cleaning spray and a clean cloth usually work, but you could also try hot, soapy water with a splash of vinegar. A ball of scrunched-up newspaper is all you need to wipe it dry, and it will leave the surface smear-free.

left Metal can be a very masculine material, with its sharp edges and uncompromising, industrial look. Metal staircases were once only seen in offices or factories, but are now a feature of the urban loft.

right Metal can also be used in a more domestic setting, as a splashback in a kitchen, where shiny foil has both practical and decorative appeal.

heavy metal

Tom Dixon used salvaged scrap metal to make his early furniture designs. 'I wasn't interested in being a designer as much as I was interested in welding,' he says. 'I used scrap metal because it was the easiest and cheapest thing available.' He took up welding at a friend's workshop as something to do during the day. In those days, his nights were spent working as a night-club promoter.

116

love 6

create 10

indulge 20

dress 66

share your home

imagine 168

We are social animals. Our homes are a shared experience. From the beginning, our homes are defined by the people we share them with, be they our parents, our siblings, our pets or even our room mates. Home life is all about fighting over who gets into the bathroom first in the morning; who holds on to the remote control; whose stereo is the loudest; and who takes up the most space on the sofa.

Family homes can be battlefields, with constant skirmishes over territory. And it doesn't end there. We move out to share a house with friends or fellow students, or to set up home with someone we love. Then, not only do we have children ourselves, we also invite our ageing parents – the ones we did battle with for most of our adolescence – to move in. And they bring their bad-tempered cat or flea-ridden dog with them. Space within the home is constantly under siege, and how we use it to accommodate friends and family needs careful consideration.

Until the 1960s, houses were designed to be very compartmentalized. Kitchens and dining rooms were separate (sometimes only linked by a hatch through which mother could pass out plates of food to the waiting diners). The living room was the place to watch television. Children had a separate playroom, or their own bedroom, where they could play without disrupting the rest of the family. And there were lots of doors. Towards the end of the 1960s and into the 1970s, open-plan living became more fashionable, with kitchens and dining rooms combined, allowing mother to keep an eye on the kids as she cooked. And if friends came round for dinner, the cooking became part of the social experience. Mother was no longer locked away in her own private compartment, with the stove, the sink, the washing machine and the ironing board. Social stereotypes were being knocked down along with dividing walls and doors. Then, with the advent of loft living in the

1980s, walls were swept away. Often, the kitchen, living room and bedroom would all be arranged within one big, free-flowing space. And this open-plan living has not been restricted to warehouse apartments. Even owners of traditional Victorian terraces and 1930s semis have caught the demolition bug, knocking down walls wherever it is possible without the roof falling in. The result is a traditional exterior and an airy, modern space within.

The house of the architect John Pawson is a perfect example. From the outside, his house is Victorian. But step inside and there are clean lines, concrete stairwells, big, open spaces and a kitchen and eating area that flows perfectly into a garden which might as well be another room. And while being a home for children and family, as well as a place to entertain friends, Pawson's house is also a retreat – a calm, soothing place to hide away from the busy madness of the outside world.

The new open approach to living makes it much easier to be more sociable within the home. It also means that our living spaces are far more fluid and flexible. We might do homework or our household accounts at the kitchen table, play music in the lounge, surf the Web on the sofa and watch television in the kitchen. And when friends come round to visit, it is much easier for both guests and host to circulate around the space without feeling as though they have to stay rooted to their chairs.

Family life is also much more on display. If we are happy living with our children's toys and mess, they tend to get integrated into the home. Some parents – often those who haven't quite grown up themselves – make their living rooms into playrooms for all the family, complete with table tennis, game consoles, tricycles and – in the case of designer and TV presenter Wayne Hemingway – an entire climbing wall. In his country home, a modernist industrial-looking chunk of a house designed by his wife, Gerardine, the first floor is a huge open-plan living/playing/eating/working space. The ground floor is for quieter activities, such as sleeping and bathing, and for access to the garden. But upstairs there is space for the children to ride their bikes and play with their friends and for adults to cook, socialize, eat and – if things don't get too noisy – listen to music or watch television. Sharing is what this home is all about.

Of course, sharing your home – and your treasured possessions – is not always easy, especially if you are not fortunate enough to have a purpose-built home designed with your needs in mind. Most of us make do with what we've got. From childhood, many of us have had to share bedrooms with siblings. Sometimes we even have to share a bed, or at least a bunk bed, so the battle lines are drawn early on. And this snug situation can continue when we have families of our own. Some couples have their first baby when they are still living in their first homes – a studio or

left Habitat catalogues from the 1970s offer an insight into the way we used to live. Eating around the table was a common shared family experience before the advent of TV dinners. Of course, you had to have the right lampshade over the dining table.

right Sharing can be fun, as well as cutting down on costs. As property prices soar in cities, friends are buying or renting together. In overcrowded capitals such as London, it is rare for a young, single person to live alone.

'A home to me is something that rises way above consumerism. Its value is more in emotional capital rather than financial capital. Our homes are places where we can be ourselves and not have to be on parade. The utopian side of me wants everyone to have had homes like mine which simply bring back happy memories and are great places for family life.'

Wayne Hemingway, fashion designer

one-bedroom apartment. When space is at such a premium there isn't much room for privacy. The kitchen, living room, bedroom and nursery flow into each other. But people can make even the most restricted of situations work for them, and some brave souls even manage to entertain. Having friends around a small fold-up kitchen table makes supper an informal but lively affair. For some, this fluid approach continues as the family grows. A home office might be squeezed in next to the cot in the nursery. The parents' bedroom might be the base camp for a continuous round of bed-hopping, as children struggle to learn the important life skill of sleeping through the night. We haven't reached the stage of nineteenth-century factory workers, who finished the night shift then jumped into the beds of family members clocking on to the day shift, but the demise of the traditional nine-to-five working pattern has forced us to be more flexible in how we organize our homes.

Often, problems come when couples move in together. This is the ultimate test of any relationship. How do you reconcile one person's taste and likes and dislikes with another's? Compatibility in love doesn't necessarily mean a mutual taste for flock wallpaper or shag-pile rugs. One might like clutter; the other might be positively allergic to 'things' around the house. A certain amount of delicate diplomacy is necessary, and often a compromise will take months to achieve. It's all about give and take: a clear-out, and the odd garage sale will help pave the way.

But it's not just couples who have problems. As property prices continue to rise, there is a growing trend for friends to rent or buy houses together. Once the mortgage has been signed, decorating a home that is serving both as an investment and a temporary stopgap is more of a science than an art. Your own rooms can be as personal as you want them to be. If you have a taste for bright colours or crystal chandeliers and ornate frames, this is the place to put them. For the communal areas, it is best to respect each other's differences and go for something neutral. That way, it will be easier to sell when the time comes, too.

For some of us, however, home life is not about friends or family, noise or mess. It is about refuge, privacy and a place to call our own. When the world outside is polluted and stressful, our inner sanctum can be a welcome refuge, a place to indulge ourselves, take stock and have time to think. It is important that even the busiest homes have somewhere to hide and be on our own. Usually, that place is the bathroom, the one room in the home where you can seek refuge behind a looked door to run a bath, listen to music, light some candles and enjoy a good soak, or read a book in peace. Perhaps that's why bathrooms have become a focal point for a bit of luxury. Who doesn't dream of a sunken bathtub, underfloor heating, exotic fragrances and some atmospheric lighting? Once you're there, this is your space. You don't have to share it with anyone (unless you want to). It's calm. It's peaceful. Just bliss.

eat

right Spaces within the home where you can cook, eat, entertain and socialize are become increasingly blurred. Kitchens work best when they are open, with room for a table and, if you are lucky, outdoor space as well.

The focus of the home has changed over the years. The television has replaced the hearth and the kitchen has become the place where the family spends most of its time – eating, drinking, cooking, socializing, partying. Our kitchens have become more sophisticated and increasingly more professional so that we have stoves that would not look out of place in a restaurant kitchen. Our cookery books reflect our taste for food from around the world.

In the past, we would move into a new home and the kitchen would be part of the fixtures and fittings. We would never have dreamed of ripping the existing one out and buying a new one. But now, our kitchens are an extension of our taste. We install the biggest, coolest-looking oven we can afford – or fit in the space available. Like a car, it's a status symbol. We buy the best possible kitchen we can, one that not only functions well, but looks good, too. From the worktops to the colour of the cupboard doors, from our toasters to our lemon squeezers, our kitchens are another way of expressing who we are. The amount of money we are prepared to spend simply emphasizes the importance we place on this room within our home. It's partly to do with the rise of the celebrity chef and the fact that we're all *au fait* with a bit of rocket (arugula) and some balsamic vinegar. Food has become much more central to the way we live – even if it is just a case of warming something up in the oven. If the oven looks impressive enough, who would know you didn't bake it yourself?

archetypes

brown betty teapot

The traditional Brown Betty teapot is said to make the best possible pot of tea. The first ceramic teapots were made towards the end of the seventeenth century, out of red clay from Stoke-on-Trent, in Staffordshire. In 1884 the Ashwood company first produced the classic round, glazed Betty teapot. Still made in the British Midlands, their design has remained unchanged to this day. Exported around the world, the affectionately named Brown Betty has become an everyday classic. It's cheap, it's basic and there is nothing to better it for a good pot of tea.

juke glass sugar pourer

From American diners to English greasy spoons, the glass sugar pourer with its metal spout is an absolute classic. You don't even think about it as you reach over to pour the required sugar fix into your tea or coffee. It's a design that just works – more hygienic than the sugar pot that everyone can dip into, and so satisfying in the way the sugar pours out like liquid.

how to make the perfect cup of tea

It's the subject of hot debate. Should you put the milk in before the hot tea, or after? In George Orwell's essay *A Nice Cup of Tea*, he advocated pouring the milk in after the tea. Some swear it should be the other way round, while purists say there should be no milk at all. The famous teashop Betty's of Harrogate has even gone so far as to publish a manual on the subject. If you follow their golden rules, you can't really go wrong:

1. Use freshly drawn water so there is plenty of oxygen still in it.
2. Warm your pot with a little water taken from the kettle.
3. Use loose tea leaves rather than tea bags. Allow one teaspoon per person and one for the pot.
4. Once the water has reached a rolling boil, pour it over the leaves. Stir well, then put the lid back on the pot.
5. Leave to infuse for at least five minutes before pouring.
6. Provide a tea strainer and stand to catch the drips.
7. Add milk, before or after the tea.

love your home

Marco Jerrentrup, chef, with Alexander, butcher's apron from Habitat
'I love this flat. It's light and versatile and there are lots of hidden nooks tucked away. It's mysterious and it works. The whole idea is that it should function; it has to work as a home. The baby centres it. I remember when he was just born, having him in one arm and baking a loaf of bread and a cake for his exhausted mother – all by 7am.'

bialetti moka express

This simple aluminium coffeepot was designed by Alfonso Bialetti in 1933. He was first inspired in the 1920s by local washerwomen who used tubs with a central pipe to draw the soapy water up and redistribute it over the washing. A true Italian coffee addict, he worked out how this steamy method could be applied to coffee-making. The company estimate that they have sold over 300 million pots, and almost 90 per cent of Italian homes are said to own at least one Bialetti product. A recent survey of Italian design put the Moka Express at number five, just behind the Vespa, the Fiat 500, and – at number one – Nutella. It is even on display at New York's Museum of Modern Art.

Bialetti set out to make espresso at home, just like it was made in the local coffee bars. His machine was compact and simple, and you didn't require any skill to make the perfect espresso. To begin with, he sold it himself from market stalls, selling around 10,000 per year from 1936 to 1940. His son, Renato, took over the marketing of the Moka after World War II and, realizing its potential, he started a full-scale, national advertising campaign. In 1953 he invented the *omini con i baffi* (the little man with the moustache) who became the trademark of the pot. It was a caricature of Alfonso. The design is unchanged to this day, and, although production methods have been modernized, the bottom boiler is still handmade by skilled workers.

arabika cups and saucers

The best way to drink espresso is from thick porcelain – such as the classic Italian Illy cups that are used in every coffee bar from Rimini to Rome. The smooth, rounded porcelain keeps the coffee hot and makes knocking back your caffeine all the more satisfying.

how to make the perfect espresso

1 Fill the base with water up to the safety valve.
2 Insert the filter funnel, and fill with coarsely ground coffee.
3 Screw the top section to the base and place over a low heat.
4 Espresso is best served in a thick ceramic cup to keep the heat in. Italians always add sugar.
5 It's recommended that you don't clean the pot too thoroughly, as the residue is thought to add to the depth of flavour.

the world in your bowl

You can see from the shelves of the local supermarket how very adventurous we have become in our eating habits. Immigration, far-flung holidays abroad, celebrity chefs and an explosion of new restaurants celebrating food from around the globe have all contributed to changing our tastes from the conservative to the cosmopolitan. We think nothing of filling our shopping baskets with pasta, pizza, korma, tortillas, papaya, green curry, galangal, rice, noodles and hoi-sin sauce. It is amazing to think that only 50 years ago, we were only just emerging from the after-effects of wartime rationing and food shortages.

When Habitat started selling woks in 1966, the average British housewife would not have known what to do with it. These days, stir-fries are as much a part of daily cooking as bacon and eggs. How quickly things have changed. Along with our shopping lists of exotic ingredients, we need the right equipment to get results. Increasingly, we eat from bowls, not plates; choose rice instead of potatoes; and reach for fresh ginger instead of pepper. The twenty-first-century kitchen is a melting pot of woks, balti pans, fondue sets, chopsticks, noodle bowls and bento boxes. We no longer have to go to Tokyo for a sushi mat. Whatever we want to eat or drink, the world is at our doorstep.

how to care for your wok

The wok is now as commonplace in kitchens as the old-fashioned frying pan or skillet. The secret of cooking with a wok is to keep it hot, and keep the food moving. Always add oil to a hot wok that is close to smoking. And you only need a small amount – this is not a deep-fryer. Experts recommend peanut (groundnut) oil. Certainly, it's a waste of olive oil. The blacker the wok, the better the results. It needs to be kept well seasoned. You simply brush the surface with oil, heat the wok then cool it again before adding another layer of oil and repeating the process. After a while, your wok will have worked up a lovely black coating that will act as its own non-stick surface. Until the wok turns completely black, wash it only with water and no soap. The best way to dry it is by heating it over the stove rather than wiping it with a towel. Season your wok again by burning oil onto the surface before putting it away. This will prevent it from rusting.

left and right Our eating habits reflect our increasingly exotic holiday destinations, from the Scandinavian fondue – a 1970s favourite revived and perfect for an evening with friends – to the Japanese sushi and miso soup. We even have the low tables and bowls to match.

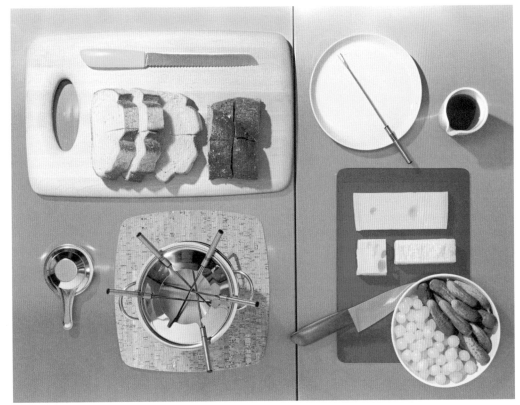

chocolate fondue

Instead of Emmental or gruyère, why not try a chocolate fondue for dessert?

300ml (½ pint) double (heavy) cream
350g (12oz) best-quality chocolate, chopped into small pieces
a good splash of rum or brandy

Heat the cream over a low heat for a couple of minutes. Add the chocolate and rum, and stir until the chocolate has just melted. Transfer to a ceramic fondue dish, and serve with strawberries, slices of apple, chunks of pineapple and sponge fingers.

formal dining

Few of us sit down for dinner at a table every day. But formal dinner parties can make an occasion special. It's all about dressing up – both for your guests and your table. The food you serve is important, but presentation is everything. A white tablecloth, crisp napkins and plain white plates make an elegant supper or a lavish Sunday lunch. But there are varying degrees of formality. It is a little old-fashioned to be faced with a daunting quantity of confusing cutlery – butter knives, fish knives and more glasses than you can hold with two hands. Usually, people are happy to hold onto their cutlery between courses. And silver service is definitely out, unless, of course, you happen to live in a stately home and have servants on hand to grapple with the peas, not to mention the washing-up.

below A formal dinner can be as fun and decadent or as sensible as you like. For a family lunch, go for simplicity.

right If you are inviting friends for dinner to show off your culinary skills, lavish the table with candles, flowers and your best china.

how to lay a table

Even formal dining is more relaxed in its approach these days; the emphasis is on allowing guests to relax rather than intimidating them. But there are some basic rules to facilitate comfortable dining:

- Forks are placed on the left, knives should be on the right. Cutlery is placed to the sides of the plate in the order it will be used. The ones furthest from the dish – for example the soup spoon – will be used first. The blade of the knife should be turned inward.
- The dessert fork and spoon are placed horizontally above the plate, the fork nearest the plate with its handle on the left and the spoon above, with its handle on the right.
- A butter knife should be placed with the butter dish. Guests should use it only to transfer butter from the dish to their plates, then use their own knife to spread it.
- For drinks, supply a water glass, a small glass for white wine and a larger glass for red wine. If there is dessert wine or champagne, add another glass or a flute on the end.
- Name cards and menus are not necessary – they are too fussy. But after all that trouble, a thank you card from the guests is always appreciated!

left No need to dress for dinner. Flip-flops (thongs) are just fine for a meal in the kitchen.

below Supper around the coffee table is an easy option after a hard day's work.

below right Oriental bowls and crockery elevate a more casual approach to dining.

informal dining

TV dinners do not have to be antisocial, lazy affairs. The reality is, eating on our laps in front of the television is the way most of us eat, most of the time. We enjoy being able to be sloppy in our own homes. We eat standing up in the kitchen. We eat straight from the container. The table is no longer a prerequisite for a meal, whether breakfast, lunch or dinner. Sometimes, after a long day at work, a take-away (take-out) is the only choice, even if you've invited friends for dinner. Nobody minds being served a ready-prepared supper in the middle of the week, although a little imagination and creativity can elevate an oven-ready meal. Pasta from the deli can be made to look trattoria fabulous with the addition of some of your own tomatoes roasted in the oven with some olive oil and sea salt. A rustic loaf of bread helps for mopping up juices. And a cheese board, with a generous bunch of grapes and some crackers takes seconds to prepare, but looks glamorous and appetizing.

TV dinner parties are an increasingly popular and easy way to catch up with both friends and the latest must-see television programme at the same time. One New York fashion designer has them on a weekly basis. The guests arrive, the food is delivered and everyone settles down for a night in front of the box. Who can resist?

archetypes

milly pepper grinders

This ubiquitous pepper grinder is the one used by the typical Italian pizzeria waiter. 'Pepper?' he asks, and from behind his back he pulls the biggest pepper mill you've ever seen. A few grinds are all you need. Traditionally, it comes in black and natural wood, but Habitat couldn't resist giving it a modern twist with new shades of pillar-box red and duck-egg blue.

canteen glasses

Millions of people around the globe cannot be wrong. Duralex toughened glass is used everywhere, from school canteens to bijoux bistros. The classic design, used for wine, water, coffee, tea or anything else you care to put in it, has been unchanged for over 35 years. It is the definitive glass – no fuss, no nonsense, stackable, functional and stylish, too. And best of all, while they don't quite bounce when you throw them, they are almost unbreakable.

eating outdoors

When the weather is fine, eating outside is one of life's greatest pleasures. There's something about eating a sandwich by the sea, or a sardine fresh from the barbecue in the garden, that makes it taste all the more delicious. There is nothing like fresh air to sharpen the appetite. But the secret to successful dining alfresco is planning. A fully equipped picnic basket makes life much easier. Everything you need is there, from your gingham tablecloth (a must for any self-respecting picnic lover) to your smoked salmon sandwiches and your flask of tea or coffee. If it's a hot day (and what more could you ask for?), then a cool box or thermos flask will keep the drinks chilled.

For the perfect barbecue, it's all in the preparation. Marinade the fish or meat in advance. Thread skewers of prawns (shrimp) and vegetables. Toss salads. Make your own relish. And don't forget to lay the table – as informally as you like – with everything you will need. A stack of paper napkins will come in handy. The barbecue itself should be just smouldering nicely to ensure that all your hard work doesn't end up as charred as charcoal.

quick avocado salsa

1 ripe avocado, diced
a few spring onions (scallions), chopped
1 tbsp olive oil
juice of 1 lime
2 tomatoes, chopped
a bunch of coriander (cilantro), chopped
salt and pepper

Mix everything together and keep it in the refrigerator until ready to serve. It tastes better if you make it a few hours in advance.

right Eating alfresco has a charm all of its own, whether it's eggs and bacon after a hard night's camping, or a picnic on a sunny day. Food always tastes better outdoors.

lounge

right Our living rooms are the most sociable rooms in the house – and the most relaxed. This is the place to curl up in front of the TV, or jump for joy when your team scores.

The living room is the room in the house where everybody meets. It is the most open, sociable room, and also the most relaxed. This is where we might read the papers with a cup of tea, chat with our friends, talk on the phone, send e-mails, put our feet up and watch television, or even have an afternoon nap. Central to the living room is the sofa. For some, this is a design statement. But it must also be comfortable, long enough to slouch on and deep enough to accommodate the longest legs. In partnership with the sofa is a coffee table – essential for snacks, books and drinks. And then there is the floor. Increasingly, we use the floor for lounging and relaxation. We lie on it to watch television. We sit on it to eat, using a low table, Japanese style. We slump on the sheepskin rug in front of the fire. A little comfort doesn't go amiss. Carpets, rugs and big cushions all make a hard floor that much more inviting.

How we relax at home depends a lot upon the seasons. In the dark, cold wintry nights, we want to hibernate with comforting bowls of pasta, warm slippers and soft blankets. In the summer, we open the windows, hang out on the balcony to cool off and watch the world go by, or open up the doors onto the garden and look at the stars.

As well as being a place to slouch, the living room is undergoing a transformation into an all-singing, all-dancing movie theatre. Advances in technology mean that home cinemas are a reality, complete with big plasma screens, popcorn and ice cream. All from the comfort of an armchair.

left and right Whether we're watching TV, organizing our social lives or simply hanging out with the pet dog, our lounges are the places for comfort and relaxation. There should be enough room to stretch out and make yourself at home.

archetype

chesterfield sofa

The chesterfield sofa is at home everywhere and anywhere. The older and more beaten up it is, the better. It's a sofa with a history. It means different things to different people, depending on their experience of it. For the British royal family, it is an heirloom, passed down from Queen Victoria and Prince Albert. For guests at London's Sanderson Hotel, it is Philippe Starck's idea of cool chic. If you are attached to the one in your local bar, it will no doubt have seen better days. It will sag in the middle. It will be scratched. It might even have a few tears. But it is like an old friend. There is something very masculine about the leather chesterfield. It also finds new life every generation or so. It has become a firm favourite with the fashion fraternity: Clements Ribeiro found theirs in a market, and it is at home in their otherwise clean, minimal house, where it looks as though it has a few stories to tell. For fashion designers Julian and Sophie, it is a part of their studio – the waiting room, reception area, the place to sit and read the papers or drink a cup of tea, and, when things get tough around collection time, the place to lie down to have a quick forty winks.

how to care for leather

The great thing about leather is that it is very good at looking after itself. It gets better with age, and the scuffs and scratches of everyday living only add to its character.

_ Do protect it from sunlight to stop it from fading and from excessive heat to prevent it from drying out.
_ Do clean it with a damp cloth or a vacuum cleaner. For stubborn marks, use a damp cloth and mild soap.
_ Do not soak leather or use cleaning fluids, wax or spray polish. Avoid chemical polishes or harsh soap.

Did you know that bulls – mainly from northern Europe – produce some of the best-quality leather? The leather is relatively unmarked by nature, as bulls don't have pregnancy stretchmarks and, of course, have very large hides.

outdoor living

The key to outdoor space – whether it's a garden, a yard, a roof terrace or a balcony – is to treat it as an extension of your home. However big or small, it is just another room. Spread out carpets and rugs on the ground, scatter cushions, serve mint tea and imagine you are in Morocco. Forget gardening. This is about living – eating, lounging, playing, entertaining and relaxing. Outdoor space is as much about decoration as indoors. If you have walls, paint them as you would the walls inside your home. Create ceilings with awnings and umbrellas. Dress your trees, hanging wind chimes, paper lanterns, fairy lights, candles and other decorations just for the fun of it. Add twinkly lights for extra atmosphere and to extend the time you can spend outdoors. And make sure there is some comfortable furniture for some serious lounging. If you have the space, a big table with benches means there is always plenty of room for family and friends.

There's nothing more luxurious than eating outdoors with a properly laid table, complete with tablecloth, freshly ironed napkins and your best china. Theme your garden parties. Pastel-coloured sun loungers can add a touch of 1970s kitsch, while old-fashioned stripy deck chairs give your garden that 1950s seaside feel. Serve drinks to match: fruit cocktails with lots of umbrellas for the loungers; homemade lemonade for the deck chairs.

easy homemade lemonade

juice of 6 lemons
150g (5 oz) sugar
1.5l (2½ pints) water

Mix the sugar with the lemon juice until it dissolves. Add the water, and serve with lots of ice and a bowl of extra sugar for those with a really sweet tooth. A chunky glass jug (pitcher) and some tall glasses are ideal for serving.

left Whether your outdoor space is a balcony, a roof terrace, a yard or a garden, it's important to make the most of it in the summer months. Eat outdoors as often as you can.

right If you don't like gardening, use decking, patios and hard land-scaping to create a low-maintenance weed- and lawn-free zone.

If you have children, there are times – possibly all the time – when your home will look like a nursery. No matter how organized you are, children's toys have a habit of taking over. In an ideal world, we would all like our own adult space that we can retreat to in the evening, away from the overwhelming tide of brightly coloured plastic and random electronic bleeps. Playrooms, or specially designated play areas within a main living room, help contain the situation, if not control it. Define an area with a mat, paint a wall with blackboard paint for mini masterpieces to be drawn in chalk, and let the kids rule their own space. Provide plenty of big containers to encourage them to stow away their toys when they've finished playing. Choose anything from a traditional wooden toybox to funky modern plastic cubes on castors, from collapsible pop-up fabric bins to huge wicker laundry hampers. If you really want to block out the mess, pull out a screen after the children have gone to bed. It will give no hint of the chaos behind.

Of course, we have to accept that our children have as much right to inhabit our space as we do, so we have to come up with some workable modes of living. All children love arts and crafts, or 'messy play'. In summer they can set up their easels in the garden, and no one worries too much about how much paint ends up on the ground. But for rainy days the kitchen is the most practical option – the flooring is likely to be able to withstand the inevitable spills. If your kitchen table is delicate, invest in a plasticized fabric sheet. They come in some great designs these days – nothing like the hideous brown oilcloths our grandmothers used to use. If your kitchen table is a little more robust, such as a pine one, you can be a little more relaxed, and simply scrub away the felt-tip pen marks once in a while, along with the red wine stains left by the grown-ups.

Nurseries can often be twee, with carefully coordinated furniture and soft furnishings. Children like a little disorder, so be bold with the decoration. Of course, they would rather be outdoors, climbing trees or playing in the sandpit.

right Children need room to spread out and play, whether indoors or out. A Scalextric track doesn't have to be confined to the playroom – it can run from room to room.

far right Outdoor space is essential if you want children to let off steam.

love your home

Sarah Featherstone, architect,
Teva lounger from Habitat
'I like the way different types of outside space relate to the rooms inside. At low level the courtyard is a jungle, a space to look at rather than be in. Plants and bamboos rise up high, so that from all levels you can see green. There are two roof terraces, one linked to the kitchen and used for outside eating, the other accessed by a bridge from the top living space, with amazing views. Wherever you are in the house you look out and beyond to other rooms, garden and sky.'

bathe

right Bathrooms have become places to spoil and pamper ourselves, with rose petals and bubble baths. The luxury spa experience has come to the home.

There was a time when bathtime simply wasn't fun. In the not-so-distant past, a bath was more of an endurance test than a pleasure. It involved tin bathtubs, draughty kitchens and pans of lukewarm water – if you were lucky. Bathtime was traditionally seen as a means to an end, not something to dwell over. Terence Conran recalls bathrooms in the 1960s as looking like prison cells. They were one step up from the outhouse, with no creature comforts whatsoever. But all that has changed. Now, not only do we have quilted toilet paper, we have designer toilets, sunken tubs, steam rooms, saunas and Jacuzzis. Twin sinks for him and her are not uncommon, with heated mirrors so they don't steam up and heated floors so the tiles are warm underfoot. Our bathrooms are now are own private spas, complete with whirlpools, fluffy towels the size of double beds, soothing lighting and all the treatments we care to indulge in, from mud wraps to exfoliating scrubs, fruity shampoos to body brushes and mineral soaks. The whole experience of taking a bath has become much more of a ritual, with the bathroom regarded as a haven, a place to relax in, unwind and pamper ourselves. We are inspired by the bathrooms we use in hotels or see in magazines, by designers such as Philippe Starck or Marc Newson, with sleek fittings, luxurious limestone floors, mosaic tiles and clean, modern lines. And if we emerge from our baths feeling revived, restored and smelling of jasmine, then bathtime has been more than just a pleasure. It has been therapy.

family bathrooms

As well as being pleasure zones, family bathrooms also serve the same function they always have – to get us clean in the shortest amount of time so that the rest of the family can get in to brush their teeth, have a shave and complete all their daily ablutions before going off for a day at school or at the office. The ideal scenario is for every family member to have his or her own en-suite bathroom, with one spare for any other emergencies or visiting guests. That way, the battle for the bathroom can be avoided. For most of us, however, it is simply a case of crowding in together, banging heads as we vie for a corner of the mirror, brushing our teeth or applying our lipstick as we go.

The family bathroom sees a lot of wear and tear, which is why floor surfaces need to be hard-wearing – rubber or tile works best. This is also probably the reason why wet rooms were invented. Nobody can complain that the floor is wet, because it is meant to be. The wet room is the ultimate in functional living. Instead of having a shower cubicle, the whole room is a shower, with a drain hole in the tiled floor to stop the whole thing turning into a paddling pool. Other fantasy family bathroom must-haves include twin sinks, a double-ended bathtub to fit two adults or several small children at once, and a hot water supply that never ends.

left The bathroom can be a battle zone for busy families trying to get to work and school in the morning. But for children, bathtime can also be playtime, with rubber ducks, toy boats and lots of bubbles.

recreational bathing

In Iceland, hot tubs are part of daily life. People meet up in the local tub to catch up on gossip and relax – just as we might meet at the local pub. Not surprisingly, the rest of the world seems to be catching on, and a hot tub in your garden is almost on a par with having your own swimming pool. They are to the noughties what the sauna was to the 1970s. And once your friends and neighbours find out, you'll become the most popular person you know.

Another garden bath treat, sure to get the neighbours' curtains twitching, is the outdoor shower. It's a water feature with a difference; you can imagine you are in the jungle or out camping. Either improvise by rigging up a basic bucket of water and a chain (for a refreshing cold shower on a very hot day) or install something a little more permanent. Perfect for exhibitionists, or if you do not have any space indoors for an extra shower.

left The outdoor shower has come a long way from the days of the outhouse. For a start, there is now hot water. These are designed for a bit of summer fun – and are perfect for those who enjoy a sense of freedom.

right Why not take a bath outside? A Jacuzzi or hot tub sunken into decking in the garden or back yard is the ultimate luxury. All you need is a heated changing room next to it. Or better still, a sauna.

sleep

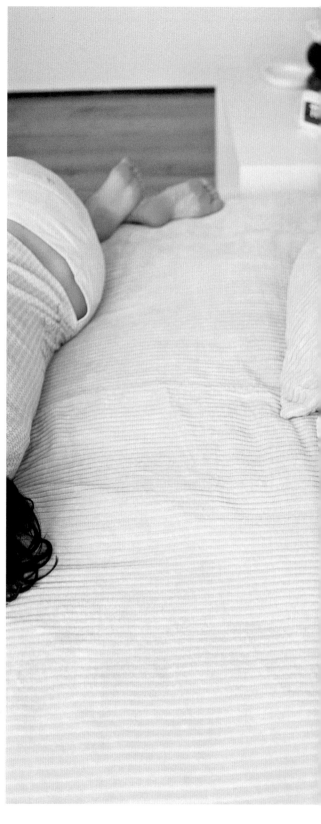

For many of us, the bedroom – or more precisely our bed – is our favourite place in the home. It's the most private, a refuge in which to unwind, relax, have sex, enjoy breakfast in bed, read the Sunday papers and, of course, sleep (not necessarily in that order). We spend more time in our beds than on our sofas, driving in our cars or sitting at the dining table. This is worth keeping in mind when investing in a new bed: it's important you get it right. Do you like your mattress hard and firm, or soft and springy? Do you like to be close to the floor or high up? Do you like to have lots of space, whether you are sharing a bed or sleeping on your own, or do you like to be cuddled up close? The only way of knowing is to try out as many as you can. Once you've decided on the comfort factor, you also need to find a bed that suits your style. A classic iron bedstead looks clean and timeless, while a futon has a certain Zen appeal.

Our beds are a refuge, warm, cosy and safe. No wonder our children like to get in with us, too. While sharing a bed with your baby is the norm across much of the world, it is still surrounded by controversy in the UK. Some experts encourage it as an essential and natural form of bonding, while others insist that babies should sleep in their own cot. What's for sure is that sharing your bed with your baby will be the beginning of a habit that might continue for years. Whether you consider it a good or a bad one depends on how well you sleep together and the size of your bed – children tend to take up as much space as they possibly can.

left and right Our bedrooms are our favourite, most private places in the home. If you keep your room minimal, clean and uncluttered, there will be less to distract you from getting to sleep. Try to avoid televisions and computers.

power naps

How much sleep we get affects how well we function during the day. According to a report in the British medical journal the *Lancet*, the average night's sleep in the UK is 90 minutes less than it was in the 1920s. The amount of sleep we need varies. Margaret Thatcher made do with just four hours a night. Napoleon said that a man needs six, a woman seven and a fool eight. (There is evidence that women need more sleep than men.) Some sleep-deprived workers resort to grabbing a catnap or – more appropriately for the workplace – a power nap, often sneaking off into the car in the carpark, under their desks or even in the toilet. In Germany, some companies have introduced sleep drop-in centres for their exhausted employees. In Spain and Italy, there is the siesta, while in China an afternoon nap is allowed by law. A report by the British think-tank Demos suggests we need to rethink our attitudes to sleep during the day, by redesigning offices with hammock bays and banning breakfast meetings at uncivilized hours.

the duvet

When Habitat introduced the duvet, or continental quilt, to the UK in the mid-1960s, it revolutionized the bedroom, not to mention the laundry. No longer were beds all about hospital corners with layers of sheets and blankets all tucked in tight to stop them coming loose in the night. The duvet brought with it an altogether more relaxed attitude. Making the bed was simply a matter of shaking out the quilt and fluffing the pillows. Even housework-shy teenagers could get the hang of it. And along with the duvet came continental breakfast, with croissants, orange juice and coffee in bed on a Sunday morning. Suddenly the bed became a place to relax, as well as a place to sleep.

The duvet is an extension of your wardrobe. Nothing else gets as close to your skin. And just like a coat or a dress, it has to suit your complexion. The colour or pattern on your duvet can affect how you sleep. Some people are sensitive to light colours and can only sleep in midnight blues or slate greys. Others swear by bright white linen, just like you get in a hotel. Certainly, a white bedroom with white sheets can make you feel clear-headed and ready for a good night's sleep. But checks, stripes, spots and florals can be fun to mix and match, and can make your room feel as inviting, modern, warm or cool as you feel.

getting a good night's sleep

_ Regular exercise helps the body to relax. But leave two hours between finishing exercise and going to bed.
_ Develop a calming ritual at night to send the right signals to your brain that it's time to wind down.
_ Going to bed and waking at regular times help the body set its own clock.
_ Avoid watching television in bed – especially if you tend to fall asleep, then have to wake up to turn it off.
_ Make sure the bedroom is a calm environment without too much clutter. Plain bed linen helps to soothe the mind.
_ Don't bring your laptop into bed with you. Save it for the office.
_ A colder bedroom is better for uninterrupted sleep. Leave the radiator off and open a window a little for some ventilation. You'll feel all the more cosy when you are snuggled up in bed.
_ Avoid too much tobacco, alcohol and caffeine in the evening.
_ Do a few drops of lavender on your pillow help you get to sleep? Research has shown that the smell increases alpha brainwaves associated with being relaxed, and helps older people to sleep better. But the same smell makes younger people restless.

left and far left When Terence Conran first introduced the duvet to the British home from Scandinavia, it caused a quiet revolution. No longer was bed-making a tedious task.

right The spare room often doubles as a bedroom for guests and the home office. A good solution is to have a day bed that can double as a sofa – perfect for the odd afternoon nap, too.

far right Bedrooms can be for more than simply getting a good night's sleep. This one has a television, music, lots of pillows, morning coffee and even a drinks tray. Everything you need for a lazy weekend in bed.

bedroom makeover

_ Giving a bedroom a new look can be as easy as buying a new set of bed linen. Go for classic white, and paint the walls to match for as clean an environment as possible. Or choose a colour scheme, and buy accessories to match the linen.

_ Paint the bedside tables and cupboard doors. Or, for extra shine, have them sprayed in gloss.

_ Change curtains (drapes). Go for colour, pattern, translucency or sparkle, whatever your mood that particular season.

_ Change your bedside light or lampshade – or simply the colour of your bulb.

love your home

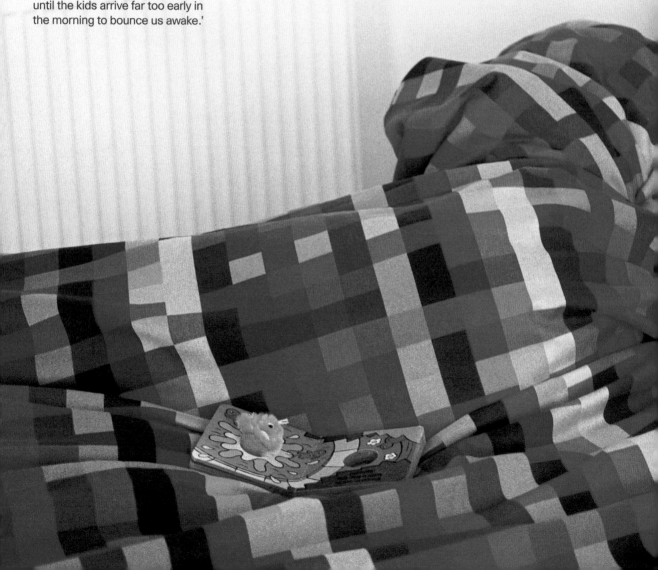

*Lucy Gowans, art director, with
her daughters, Pixel duvet cover
from Habitat*
'Having lived in a wreck for four years,
I now particularly cherish our light,
bright house. It's always a joy to
come home to. The girls love tricycling
or crawling around at speed in the
open-plan kitchen/living area, where
light floods in through a sliding glass
door that leads onto a small decked
area, which we are slowly trying to
turn into a jungle. The bedroom is
very minimal and is an oasis of calm
until the kids arrive far too early in
the morning to bounce us awake.'

168

love 6

create 10

indulge 20

dress 66

share 116

imagine your home

right Charles Deaton's
Sculptured House in
Colorado was built
in 1969, and was used
as the setting for Woody
Allen's 1973 movie,
Sleeper. When it was
first built it looked like
a UFO had landed –
and it still does today.

We cannot resist looking to the future and predicting how we will look and live a few generations on. But our ever-changing visions of the future have a strange habit of never quite becoming reality.

Certainly, in the 1960s, there was a craze for architects, fashion designers and other forward thinkers to gaze into their crystal balls. And what did they see? Lots of silver and white. Chain mail. Shiny plastic. Curves. And pods. Man was just about to walk on the moon and, for a decade at least, it seemed as though the future had arrived.

Science fiction has certainly played its part in promoting visions of the future, from *2001: A Space Odyssey* to *Barbarella* and, more recently, *Mad Max II*. The Sculptured House, for example (or the Jetson House as it has been called, after the space-age cartoon) was the work of the American architect Charles Deaton. He began building his vision of the future in Colorado. It was completed in 1969, a curvilinear structure that looked like a spaceship had landed. 'People aren't angular,' he said. 'So why should they live in rectangles?' His aim was to build a sculpture you could live in. It was such a forward-thinking structure that it was used in 1973 as the set for Woody Allen's film *Sleeper*, set in the year 2174, complete with Deaton's purpose-built podular furniture, stark white interiors and the alien-looking exterior. But the house has by no means been frozen in a futuristic time capsule. The interior was only completed according to Deaton's plans in the 1990s, and it is fitted with all the mod cons you might expect.

The Italians were leading the way in futuristic furniture design, with Joe Colombo's plastic modular interiors and Gaetano Pesce's UP series of chairs made of polyurethane

vacuum packed flat into PVC envelopes. When unpacked, they expanded to their normal size – organic, comfortable and just the thing for the ultra-fashionable modern home. In Paris, Paco Rabanne made silver and plastic chain mail body armour – a trend recently revisited on the catwalks.

Forty years on, however, we are not walking around wearing Bacofoil spacesuits. Nor do we wear silver paint on our bodies. We do not look like extras from *Star Trek*. And most of us do not live in architect-designed tributes to the ultra-modern but the same old houses we lived in then. Our furniture is made from wood. If anything, we are more interested in looking back than forward. We cling to our antiques, our vintage textile prints and our original fixtures and fittings – from the fireplaces we no longer use to the mouldings and cornices that were built into our rooms as decorative features over 100 years ago. The future is, of course, simply a continuation of what went before. We evolve. We take a few steps forward and one step back.

It is surprising how many designs from the past are still considered modern today – more modern in fact than most contemporary work. You can guarantee that any new building or space will be fitted out with every architect's favourite chair, the LC2. It fits the bill perfectly – minimal but comfortable in black leather with a tubular-steel frame. And it makes any space look cool, urbane and of the moment. It loves nothing better than a vast expanse of

glass, concrete and chrome. But the LC2 was designed by Le Corbusier in 1928. It really is a case of going back to the future; despite its near octogenarian status, the chair shows no signs of ageing. Similarly, the great sweeping Arcos lamp, designed in 1962 by Achille and Pier Giacomo Castiglioni, has become an icon of the future. Sales are greater today than they have ever been.

In many ways, it seems that we are only just catching up with the ideas and designs of the 1960s. Then, designers were driven by postwar idealism. They genuinely believed that they could make the world a better place by designing stuff that would make life easier and more harmonious. There were new materials and new techniques to explore. The world, it seemed, was an optimistic place, constantly on the brink of new discoveries and innovations.

Today, the future is still big business. Predictions agencies thrive on our need to know what's next. And to some extent, they do shape how we live, the colours we paint our walls, the shapes of our chairs and the surfaces in our kitchens. One of the leading trend forecasters today is Li Edelkoort, who advises a wide range of industries on how their products should look, feel and smell, from cars to cosmetics. A lot of it is about being confident enough to believe in what you are predicting, so that it becomes a self-fulfilling prophesy. 'We are supposed to be living this extraordinary future,' says Tom Dixon. 'Where I think we've

left Tom Dixon's mirror-ball lamp looks back to the 'yuppie' look of the 1980s with a nod to the futuristic designs of the 1960s too. Like fashion, interiors trends work in cycles. It's all about timing.

right Gaetano Pesce's UP furniture came vacuum packed flat in PVC envelopes. The 1969 publicity shots for the manufacturer, B&B Italia, put it in a lunar setting, with futuristic body-stockinged, Afro-wigged models. The furniture is still in production today.

below right The interiors for the 1968 movies *2001: A Space Odyssey* were a strangely accurate prediction, mixing antique furniture with new technology.

gone wrong is in people thinking it will be fundamentally different. And it's not. When you see how many people actually lived that plastic heaven of the 1960s, there were hardly any at all. The most iconic things at the time had tiny sales – some of them were smaller then than now. The reality is that even in your spaceship, you're going to be wanting your potted plant and your granny's antique desk, so I do think in that sense that the future isn't quite as scary as people thought it might be.'

What is for sure is that, on the journey to the future, we will go through many cycles and many reactions. Part of the art of being a predictions guru is being contrary. If pink and fluffy is in today, next year it will be black and hard. Dixon predicts a return to the 'yuppie' look of the 1980s. It's happened in fashion, so it is almost inevitable it will happen in interiors. Dixon's own mirror-ball lamp is, he says, a good example. It's hard, shiny, glitzy and cold. 'I predict a return to shoulder pads, power lighting. Maybe what's new is something cold and non-coloured,' he says. 'It's a cycle. But you get it wrong by only a year and you have a commercial disaster on your hands.'

The future is not, however, simply determined by trend predictions studios. 'You can't predict the future every time because you don't know what's going to happen, what ecological disaster, what new materials will be found,' says Dixon. Part of the catalyst to the explosion of new ideas in

the 1960s was a direct result of the space race. Designers were inspired not just by images of space craft and all the paraphernalia that went with it. They were also excited about new materials and finding new ways of using them. There was an optimism that anything was possible. What will shape the future is better glue, better materials, better technology. 'There may well be genetic engineering where you'll be able to grow furniture – grow specific shaped trees,' says Dixon. 'It's not that unbelievable.'

Of course, we are not simply cherry picking from the past to move into the future. What is exciting Dixon right now is the idea of rapid prototyping. Printers with a 3-D facility are making it possible to create products to order, on demand. 'The retail dream is that you don't make a product until people pay for it – you don't stock anything,' says Dixon, who predicts that the next move, away from the warehouse store, is stores that are factories – your furniture is made while you wait. Already, Habitat has pioneered its Art on Demand scheme: customers order their prints from a huge on-line gallery, and they are printed digitally and dispatched without fuss. 'If you can do that in furniture it means unlimited choice opens up.' People will be able to choose from a vast palette of colours, and be able to specify size and shape. The customer will, to some extent, become the designer. 'Maybe you'll have a machine that makes stuff at home,' muses Dixon. Imagine!

Technology will undoubtedly open up many new ways of designing, manufacturing and retailing. But demand for innovation is slow. Our needs are pretty much the same as they were back in 1964, when Habitat presented a range of products for the home that were useful, sometimes fashionable, usually just well designed. Terence Conran was not looking to the future, but to the needs and desires of a generation at that moment in time. But the whole idea of creating a store where you could find everything from a wooden spoon to a bed and the sheets and pillowcases to go on it was an innovation. Forty years later, the principles behind Habitat – and indeed, some of the products – remain the same. That's what we call forward thinking.

'I guess that my life experience will influence my work in the future, as it does now. The more complex our lives become, the more important our basic needs will be, such as eating, sleeping and real personal space. I am looking forward to nano technology coming to my desktop, so that I can make even smaller flowers!'

Tord Boontje, lighting and furniture designer

visions of the future

In 1956 the British architects Peter and Alison Smithson unveiled their house of the future at the *Daily Mail* Ideal Home Exhibition in London. It was designed as a plastic structure that could be mass-produced as a whole unit, complete with modular moulded shelving, low ergonomic furniture and an indoor garden. The whole thing was meant to be as low maintenance as possible, with a self-cleaning bathtub, easy-to-clean corners and remote-controlled television and lighting. Today, photographs of the prototype house make it look like a set from a science-fiction movie, complete with its alien inhabitants with silver hair and tights with built-in shoes (for men as well as women). But architects and designers are still looking to solve the same problems today – and coming up, basically, with the same answers. We have self-cleaning ovens. Remote controls are used everywhere in the home, for everything from the television to the stereo. And the idea of making whole houses that can be built off-site and simply winched into place is becoming a reality, from wooden-framed kit houses to experimental prefabricated modular homes.

Curves remain a consistent feature of futuristic design. The prolific product designer Luigi Colani imagined his Living Space of Tomorrow in 1970, and there was not a straight line in sight. 'Why should I join the straying mass who want to make everything angular?' he asks. 'I am going to pursue Galileo Galilei's philosophy: My world is also round.' Back in the 1940s, the designer and architect

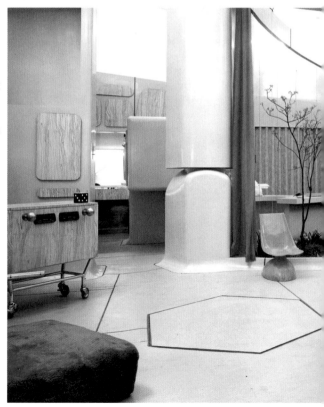

above and right These Dockable Dwelling modular houses were designed by Californian architect Matias Creimer, borrowing NASA's approach to 'space station modular docking'. His idea is a collection of modules that are prefabricated with almost no on-site assembly. You simply level up your land and plug your modules together as and when you need more space.

left The Smithsons' House of the Future was designed for the *Daily Mail* Ideal Home Exhibition in 1956 – another prefabricated unit designed to be low maintenance.

left Buckminster Fuller's Wichita House, built in 1945, was made of aluminium, way ahead of its time. It borrowed techniques and materials from mobile-home construction.

right Pierre Cardin's Bubble Palace is all about curves and circles. Built in the 1970s by Danish architect Anti Lovag, it is a wondrous series of pods and bubble-shaped rooms.

Buckminster Fuller was experimenting with geodesic domes. His 1945 domed Wichita House was made of aluminium and was designed like a mobile home. It needed no skilled labour to erect it. Similarly, the Bubble Palace, perched near Cannes on the Côte d'Azur and designed in the 1970s and 1980s by Danish architect Anti Lovag, is – as the name suggests – all about curves and circles. Just as Charles Deaton saw his house as sculpture rather than architecture, Lovag's series of interconnecting bubbles is more about lunar caves, igloos, pods and organic shapes than architecture – he calls himself a habitat-ologist. Everything about the palace, which was bought by the fashion designer Pierre Cardin in the 1980s, is curved, from the beds to the kitchen. The idea was for clients to participate in the building of their own homes, picking out pods and bubbles that they like and having them custom-made according to their own needs.

The Bubble Palace is just the sort of place in which you would imagine the Italian designer Joe Colombo to have lived, if he had lived beyond his 41 years. He devoted his short but prolific career to creating furniture for the environment of the future. His ideas were democratic – he made furniture, such as his ground-breaking Universale chair, that could be mass-produced in volume and would be available and accessible to all – but his work always looked as though it had been designed for a spaceship.

Everything, from his 1970 Boby trolley, still in production today, to his Additional Living Seating System, which was a series of rounded cushions that could be fitted together in different configurations, was shiny, synthetic and curvy. He was quite a visionary, predicting that advances in technology would allow us to work at home, and that we would need spaces that could be transformed and customized to accommodate our needs. In 1969 he designed Visiona, an entire house that was contained within a series of compact mobile elements, complete with bed, bathroom and kitchen.

compact living

right Piercy Conner's Microflat is a low-cost, prefabricated home for young urban first-time buyers. It is so compact that it was small enough to fit into the windows of London's Selfridges – complete with sitting tenants. Solutions such as this are going to be increasingly in demand as the world's cities become more crowded.

Over the next 10 years, the population of the UK will rise by 10 per cent to over 65 million. Space and resources such as electricity will become even more precious than they are now. Compact living will become a reality. Not only will generations of families have to start living together, but also our homes – in overcrowded cities at least – are going to become smaller. Already, it seems, we are running out of space. In London and other cities around the UK and the rest of the world, urban sites are being snapped up by property developers keen to build high-density housing. High-rise living will become increasingly fashionable.

Architects are having to find ways of making the most of small pockets of land which are often difficult to build on as they are already surrounded by housing or offices. London-based architects Piercy Conner have come up with a clever solution to the problem with the Microflat – a prefabricated capsule designed for a young, urban dweller in need of low-cost accommodation in inner-city London. The apartment was put on show in the window of London department store Selfridges in February 2002, complete with two inhabitants, or 'micronauts', who lived in it for a week at a time. It fitted perfectly. 'It's one solution,' says Richard Conner. The first real-life Microflats are planned for East London.

Another solution to making the most of London's ever-decreasing building land is to find ways of maximizing gaps between buildings. That is just what Joe Hagan of USE

Architects did in 2001 when he designed a house to slot between two existing buildings in London's Clerkenwell. The Gap, as the house was called, was just 3.3m (11ft) wide and 8.5m (28ft) deep, built on the site of an old minicab office. It meant there was space for just one room per floor, connected by a tiny elevator running up and down the back of the house. It takes a different mind-set to live in a house that runs vertically rather than horizontally, but the house even has a garden – a terrace on the top floor.

The idea of vertical living is one we are going to have to become used to if we are to keep up with demands on the housing market. Over the next 25 years, we need to build 3.8m new homes in the UK. And islands have a finite amount of land on which to build. Birmingham's first luxury tower block is due for completion in 2005. It is architect Ian Simpson's solution for creating 150 one- and two-bed apartments and a 220-bedroom hotel, all on a roundabout in the centre of the city. It will be 40 storeys high, but takes up a mere 550sq m (6,000sq ft) of land on the ground.

Living in small spaces can be done. Perhaps we need to look at submarines, space stations and homes in Japan, where it is perfectly normal to live in a space measured not even by metres, but by tatami mat. Japanese designer Tokujin Yoshioka has designed a typical Tokyo apartment, creating an open-plan space with all the utilities – kitchen, bathroom, storage, washing machine and so on – fitted

left Industrial Facility's 'Equipment' kitchen, designed for Whirlpool Italia and launched at the Milan Furniture Fair in 2004, is a foldaway capsule kitchen that comes complete with refrigerator, microwave, hob, steam oven, dishwasher and sink.

right Tokujin Yoshioka's redesign of the typical Tokyo apartment for Muji, the 'Muji & Infill Renovation', hides all the utilities – bathroom, kitchen and washing facilities – behind closed doors, leaving the living space clear and uncluttered.

behind sliding doors around the outside of the space. It is a lesson in minimalism, functionalism and discipline. To live here you have to keep your possessions to a minimum.

You also need a very compact kitchen, and that is what Sam Hecht and Kim Colin of Industrial Facility designed for the Italian company Whirlpool Italia. Launched at the Milan Furniture Fair in 2004, their 'Equipment' kitchen is just 2.3m (7ft) high by 1.6m (5ft 3in) wide and contains everything you might expect in a normal kitchen, including a refrigerator, electronic hob, microwave, steam oven, a dishwasher that features a three-minute cycle and, of course, a sink. Their luxurious compact kitchen is hidden behind closed doors, and you might mistake it for a large American-style fridge-freezer. It is, they say, a response to the consumer's 'revolt against conspicuous consumption'. They do not seek more products, but better ones. And the scale of the project is a solution to the 'urbanized, cerebral, high-income lifestyle'. In other words, less is more.

right Think of a doll's house. It's all about proportion. A small living space needs the same careful thought and organization. A mezzanine floor can divide a room in half horizontally, adding extra space for a bathtub or bedroom – or both, if you're lucky.

how to make the most of a small space

Making the best use of a small living space takes serious planning and organization:

_ Do make use of multifunctional furniture: tables and beds that fold up, and storage units that double as tables or chairs.

_ Do make sure your furniture is in scale with the space. A big sofa will simply dominate a room.

_ Do find clever ways of storing things. Put shelves high up on walls and over doors; use space under floors.

_ Don't try to cram too much in. Be selective. Get rid of anything you don't need. If you can't stand to get rid of something, put it into storage.

_ Do make use of hooks – they are useful for hanging everything from stools to bikes.

_ Do look out for compact bathroom and kitchen furniture. Most appliances come in small sizes.

_ Don't be afraid to knock down walls – two small, pokey rooms can be more useful than one medium-sized one.

_ Do look for space-saving ideas such as the Navona bed. Designed by Bethan Gray for Habitat, it has a mechanism that allows the mattress to lift up, revealing storage space underneath for bed linen, pillows, quilts or whatever else you need to store.

technology

Imagine arriving home to find your bath has already been drawn for you – at just the right temperature – and your supper is heating up in the oven. Your washing machine has ordered the spare part it needs and alerted the engineer, your refrigerator has ordered more milk and cheese direct from the supermarket and the lawn mower has just finished mowing the lawn. The television is ready to run a selection of your favourite programmes when you want to watch them, and your virtual picture frame has received a snapshot of your baby niece who has just taken her first steps. The lights are on, and the blinds (shades) have closed themselves. Your home is not just your home. It's your mother, lover, housekeeper and your computer, all in one. It looks after you. Or at least, it is programmed to look after you. With a little blue-tooth technology, and some other clever science and techno stuff, a home like this might be yours in the not too distant future.

For mobile (cell) phone companies such as Orange, the technology is already there. It just needs to be built into the infrastructure of your home. The Orange House of the Future looks like any suburban home. But it is super-intelligent. If you are on vacation or away on business, you will be able to access your home, turn the lights on and off, let the on-line grocery delivery in and send shopping lists to your refrigerator so that it can make sure everything is ready for when you get home. You might not be able to see the technology, but it will change the way we live. It's amazing to think that only 10 years ago mobile phones were the size of suitcases. And soon we will be able to access our homes from the palm of our hands.

Advances in technology happen almost too quickly for most of us to keep up. But the Internet and e-mail have radically transformed the way we live. For a start, it is now commonplace to have a computer at home. And they are no longer just grey boxes – they come in bright colours and are decorative as well as functional. Home offices are a relatively new phenomenon. Live/work spaces are no longer simply urban warehouses. We now live, work, eat, play and socialize in the same place. We no longer have to travel to work. We can do it from home. Distances are irrelevant. Work and home life have merged.

left, right and below
The Orange House of the Future is an exercise by the mobile (cell) phone company in creating a wireless, intelligent home. The technology is all there, but from the outside the house looks like any other. Photovoltaic tiles on the living room roof provide energy. Every member of the family has their own Web tablet to store their preferred television programmes and music, the washing machine calls the plumber when something goes wrong, and the bathtub can be programmed to fill itself to a preset temperature.

left Working at home often means setting up shop in a corner of the living room. You can divide an office space from the rest of your home with sliding doors.

right and far right Or you can organize your office equipment in a unit that hides it all away until you need to use it.

below near right Inflate's Office in a Bucket, launched in 2003, inflates in eight minutes, ready to use wherever you need a temporary office. It creates your own room within a room, perfect for a large open-plan loft space.

love your home

*Paul Tilby, graphic designer,
Surfer table from Habitat*
'My home is an ex-local authority flat
in a great location, with a community
spirit that I really enjoy. I've gutted the
interior and given the space a retro
feel with tongue-and-groove cladding
on the walls, cherry wood floors and
muted colours. The best thing about
this place are the substantial walls,
which let me indulge my love of music
without bothering the neighbours. I
can happily spend hours here updating
my iPod and browsing the Internet.'

furniture while you wait

New technology and materials will change the way products are made – and the way they will look. Alex Gabriel and Willeke Evenhuis graduated in 3-D design at the Art Academy in Arnhem in the Netherlands. Together, they have developed a series of lamps for the Belgian art and technology company Materialise that look impossible to produce. They are incredibly complex shapes, but have no seams. They look as though they have been made in one piece. The whole process is done using rapid proto-typing techniques originally developed for use in the automotive and aerospace industries. The design is done using a 3-D modelling computer programme that is then sent to a 3-D printer. The lamps are built with layers and layers of polyamide powder, melted together using lasers. The lampshade can be made while you wait. And you can order 100, or just one. The process also allows the customer to make changes, specify different sizes and be involved in the making of their product. This type of rapid prototyping is still in its early stages, but it won't be long before it is being applied to all sorts of products.

The idea of making furniture while you wait, and offering a wider choice, is one Tom Dixon himself has explored with his Fresh Fat plastic extrusions for his own company, set up in 2001. Plastic is extruded like spaghetti, then woven into shape to form chairs, tables and bowls in a choice of 100 colours. The London department store Selfridges had the Fresh Fat extrusion machine in its windows for two months, enabling customers to specify size and colour, and have their products made in front of them. Each product is unique. Although the process is high-tech and the materials are synthetic, these products are part of a new generation of techno-craft.

'It started as an experiment in future retailing,' says Dixon. 'If out-of-town shopping, where the customer goes direct to the warehouse, is the present state of shopping, then surely the next step would be to have the customer go directly to the factory. The customer is then involved in making their own product.' This is the retailer's dream scenario, where the product comes off a production line at the touch of a button, meaning there would be no need to carry unnecessary amounts of stock, and every product would be made to fulfil a customer's specific order.

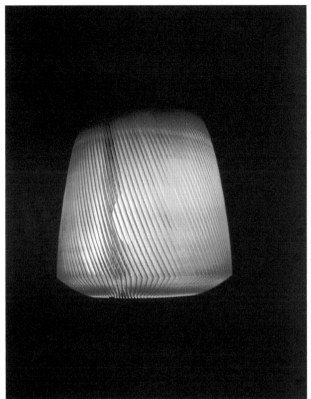

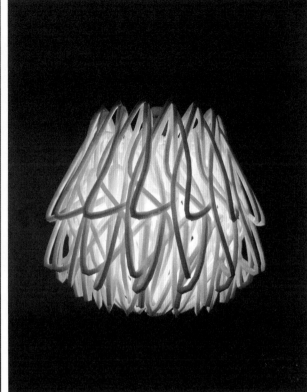

above These two lampshades are from a collection designed by Alex Gabriel and Willeke Evenhuis for the Belgian company Materialise, using rapid prototyping techniques where a design is fed into a computer and the product is made using a 3-D printer at the touch of a button.

right Tom Dixon's Fresh Fat plastic products are extruded before the customer's eyes, and can be taken home while still warm. The technique is used to make accessories and small objects as well as larger pieces like tables and chairs.

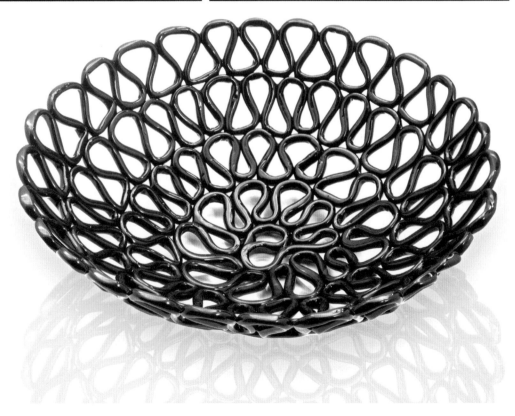

the ecological home

Environmentalists warn that we need to act now if we are to avert – or at least postpone – a future planet-wide ecological crisis, and the best place for most of us to start is at home. It can be as simple as turning on an energy-saving light bulb. You might not feel as though you are doing much, but if everyone else did the same it would be one less drain on our precious energy resources.

Slowly, more designers and architects are becoming increasingly committed to the cause, advocating the use of green materials and sustainability. But as the problem becomes more acute, and as the European Union passes more directives, building eco-friendly houses will no longer be a choice but the law. The British architect Bill Dunster is leading the way forward with his ideas on zero-energy development. At his celebrated BedZED housing project in Beddington, Sutton, the environment and sustainability were central to the design and build. It is the world's first high-density carbon-neutral housing development. It uses energy only from renewable resources generated on site. Tree waste that would otherwise go to landfill is used to generate power to supplement solar power. A car pool uses electric cars. And water consumption is radically reduced by the use of dual-flush toilets and spray taps, and by the collection of rainwater from the roofs which is used for flushing toilets and irrigating the development's sky gardens. Not surprisingly, BedZED was a runner-up in

the 2003 Stirling prize, awarded by the Royal Institute of British Architects. It has become a benchmark to which other builders and developers can aspire. Dunster has shown what is possible. And in the future, developments like BedZED will be the only way forward for new housing.

Other innovative ideas in environmentally friendly housing include architect Sarah Wigglesworth's internationally acclaimed home in north London, which uses straw bales, recycled concrete and sandbags, as well as rainwater recycling and composting toilets. On a larger scale, the Solaire building in New York has become the first high-rise residential block to use photovoltaic (PV) panels and other green technology. The 30-storey building, near Battery Park, uses PV tiles as part of the fabric of the building – on the walls, roof and the entrance canopy.

left Bill Dunster's BedZED housing project is a zero-energy housing development that uses energy from renewable sources generated on site. The combination of super-insulation, a wind-driven ventilation system incorporating heat recovery, and passive solar gain stored within each apartment by thermally massive floors and walls, reduces the need for both electricity and heat. This is the future of housing if we are to keep up with EU directives on energy consumption and sustainability.

right The SkyZED Flower Tower is Bill Dunster's concept for a mixed-use tower community, built on a tight urban site. The tower is designed to generate its own energy and to optimize views, daylight and privacy to all apartments. The plan has four petal-shaped floor plates arranged like an open flower.

left Buildings can merge sympathetically with the natural surroundings – and in some cases even incorporate nature into the framework of the house.

right Japanese architect Shigeru Ban uses fully biodegradable cardboard to make entire buildings – from galleries to temporary shelters for use in emergencies such as earthquakes, or to provide shelter for homeless refugees.

eco materials

Today, it is not possible to live a perfectly ecologically sound existence. But of course, we can do our bit where it helps. We can recycle our glass and paper. We can choose eco-friendly materials such as rubber, Marmoleum, cork and bamboo for our floors. We can paint our walls using low-emissions paints, and use organic cotton and recycled materials wherever possible. Kitchen worktops, for example, can be made from anything and everything, from recycled drink bottles to plastic bags. In Japan, the architect Shigeru Ban specializes in making entire buildings out of cardboard, applying the same techniques to refugee shelters as to galleries for fashion designers such as Issey Miyake. And in the UK, children at Westborough Primary School in Westcliff-on-Sea, Essex, have an after-school club made out of their own recycled card and paper. It is made out of 90 per cent recycled materials and is itself 90 per cent recyclable at the end of its 20-year life. Within the home, cardboard can be used to make furniture (the acclaimed architect Frank Gehry produced a series of low-cost cardboard furniture in the 1970s) or simply re-used to make necessities such as storage boxes. Habitat's Cargo boxes are made from recycled cardboard reinforced with metal rivets and corners to make them strong and durable.

how to make your home more eco-friendly

For those of us who live in old-fashioned, draughty, energy-wasting houses, making our homes even a bit greener can seem like an impossible task. But we can do our best to recycle our garbage, compost our kitchen waste and insulate our homes. It is not simply a matter of buying a wind-up radio – but every little bit helps. We can ensure that our furniture is made from renewable sources of wood. We can look for eco-friendly alternatives when choosing flooring – linoleum, rubber, bamboo laminates. We can repair things, rather than simply throwing them away. And we can support designers who are using greener materials, or recycling and reinterpreting existing ready-made products to make new ones.

It's all very easy – although very expensive – to buy organic vegetables at the supermarket or to shop for fresh produce at your local farmers' market. But whatever happened to the 1970s dream of self-sufficiency and living off your own small patch of land? Perhaps we are all too short of time to go out digging manure and planting potatoes. Or perhaps we just don't have the land. Window boxes are great places to grow herbs, but they do have their limitations. For serious gardeners, allotments or gardening cooperatives are the perfect solution, and they are becoming increasingly fashionable among a younger generation. There is something incredibly satisfying about planting a row of seeds and digging up a bountiful supply of exotic lettuce leaves a few months later. If you plant them in succession, you will have enough to keep you – and all your family and friends – in salad for the entire summer. But allotments are only for the committed. They might provide you with fruit and veg for most of the year, but they also keep you busy. A good idea is to share an allotment with a friend or to rent half a plot. That way, the task won't feel too daunting, and you won't be left with enough beans and courgettes (zucchini) at the end of the summer to set up your own market stall.

eco tips

- Choose a bin that divides your rubbish into different compartments – glass, paper, compost and such like. Recycling your waste is simply a matter of filing.
- Don't waste electricity. Turn off lights when you're not using them. Try to use energy-saving bulbs.
- Don't waste water.
- Use a clothes line rather than an electric clothes dryer. Your clothes will smell much fresher, too.
- Invest in a domestic wind turbine and create your own mini wind farm. These small-scale turbines can be fixed to individual chimneys, and they can provide up to 15 per cent of a household's annual electricity needs. If you want more information, go to www.windsave.com.
- Clad your roof in photovoltaic (PV) tiles. They look smart – light years away from the traditional solar panel – and on an average house will generate enough energy to save half a tonne of carbon dioxide a year. In Germany, more than 10,000 houses have been fitted with PV tiles over the past 10 years.

right Living the good life can be an eco-friendly fantasy. Recycling your waste, growing your own greens and making sure our homes and furniture are built from sustainable materials is almost a full-time job in itself. But every little bit helps.

left Paper Mountain is a modern take on the pouf, designed by J M Ferrero. You simply fill it with your crumpled-up newspapers and magazines. The outer shell is made from a biodegradable plastic.

compost

It is not until you start a compost heap that you realize how much household refuse is green. You significantly reduce the amount of material left out for refuse collection if you take out the biodegradable matter and leave it to rot in your own compost bin.

How to make perfect compost
1 Start your compost heap directly on the ground so that the worms have easy access.
2 Begin with a layer of coarse material and build up with layers of garden and kitchen waste.
3 Make sure the heap is always moist.
4 When the heap starts to shrink and cool, take out the contents and shake up the compressed matter and add it back into the heap.
5 Your compost is ready for use when it is brown and crumbly in texture.

What you can add
_ Kitchen scraps – but no meat or cooked foods, unless you want to attract rats and other vermin.
_ Old wool and cotton clothes cut up into small pieces and soaked in water.
_ Wood ash.
_ The contents of your vacuum-cleaner bag.

love your home

Nora Doerfel, dressmaker,
Eco pots from Habitat
'Gardening is a great way of doing
your bit for the planet. I like to do what
I can. I keep a compost bin for kitchen
and garden waste, and I have an
allotment up the road where I grow
vegetables – onions, potatoes, green
beans, tomatoes and salad leaves.
In the summer, there are plums and
blackberries for jam. I like these pots
because they will decompose back
into the earth eventually. They might
even end up on my compost heap.'

index

Figures in italics refer to captions

A

2001: A Space Odyssey (film) 170, *174*
Aalto, Alvar 107
Additional Living Seating System 178
Allen, Woody 170, *170*
allotments 198
aluminium 112, 178, *178*
archetypes 17, 18
  Arabika cups and saucers 130-1
  Baletti Moka Express 130-1
  blue and white Cornish kitchenware 44-5
  Brown Betty teapot 126-7
  café tablecloth 94-5
  canteen glasses 138-9
  chesterfield sofa 146-7
  Juke glass sugar pourer 126-7
  Michael Thonet's bentwood furniture 48-9
  Milly pepper grinders 138-9
Architropolis 71
armchairs 142
  'Vienna' 48
Arnhem Art Academy 192
art deco 96
Art on Demand scheme (at Habitat) 174
ashtrays: Clam Ashtray 38, *39*
Ashwood company 126
Astoria restaurant, Trondheim 71
Atfield, Jane 34
avocado salsa, quick (recipe) 140

B

Baldele, Georg *54*
bamboo 197, 198
Ban, Shigeru 196, 197

Barbarella (film) 170
barbecues 140
Bardot, Brigitte 40
bathrooms 12, 71, 72, 74, 102, 123, 154-9, 180, *182*
  family 156-7
  recreational bathing 158-9
baths 104, 123, 154, 157, 176, *187*
Bauhaus 18, 112
beams 72
bed frames *105*
bed linen *63*, *82*, *93*, 164, 184
bedrooms 72, 74, *90*, 109, 118, 120, 123, 160-67
  makeover 164
beds 17, 30, 109, 120, 123, 160, *164*, 184
  Navona 184
BedZED housing project, Beddington,
  Sutton 194, *195*
benches 148
Bialetti, Alfonso 130
Bialetti, Renato 130
Bialetti Moka Express 130
Biba 16
bins (trash cans) 112, 150, 198
Birmingham 180
Blahnik, Manolo 25
blankets 25, 30, 35, 58, *101*, 109, 142
blinds (shades) 164, 186
book endpapers 101
bookcases 51, 60
books 88
bookshelves 60
Boontje, Tord 58, *59*, 175
  Wednesday project 58
bowls 76, 132, *133*, *136*, 142, 192
boxes
  Cargo 65, 197

filing 92
storage 60, 61, 63, 65, *65*
Broadhurst, Florence *90*, 99
brooms 34, *36*
brushed steel 104
brushes 25, 34
Bubble Palace, near Cannes 178, *178*
Buckminster Fuller, Richard 178, *178*
butcher's apron *128*

C
cabinets, display 60
cable ties 52, *52*
calico 104
Calyx print (Lucienne Day) 96, *97*
candles *134*, 148
  Turned Candle 25–6
cardboard 104, 197
  biodegradeable *196*
  recycled 197
Cardin, Pierre 178, *178*
carpets 12, 71, 72, 102, 109, 142, 148
cashmere 30, 109
Castelli Ferrieri, Anna 65, *65*
Castiglioni, Achille 172
Castiglioni, Anna 38
Castiglioni, Pier Giacomo 172
Central School of Arts and Crafts, London 12, 38
ceramics 96
chairs 25, 72, *78*, *86*, 104, 172, 192
  675 dining chair 38
  Ant 46
  Bauhaus 112
  bentwood 48, *48*
  Eames Lounger 46
  LC2 172, *172*
  Number 14 48
  Polyprop 46, *47*
  reading 25
  rocking 48
  rush-seated kitchen 17
  Universale 178
  UP series 170, 172
chandeliers 123
  Blossom 58, 59
  'Milk Bottle' *54*
checks 92, 94, *98*, 101, 162
Chelsea set 12, 16
chests of drawers *63*
chicken brick *18*
children's play 150–51
china 16, *33*, 88, 94, *134*, 148
chintz *90*, 99
chocolate fondue (recipe) 133
Chow, Mr 26
chrome 71, 112, 172
cladding *107*, 190
Clements Ribeiro 146
Clerkin, Carl 28, *28*
clock, Mariner 26, 40, *41*
clothes lines 198
clutter 26, 28, 60, *65*, 123
coat hangers 17, 26
coat hooks *28*
coat stands 28, 48, *51*
Cocksedge, Paul 52, *54*
coffeepots 130
Colani, Luigi 176
Cole & Son *90*, 99
Colin, Kim 182
collage *71*, 88
Colombo, Joe 170, 178
colour 68, 71, 72, 74–87, 101

colours of the world 76–7
cool colours – light and shade 84–5
  neutrals with an accent 78–9
  primary colours 74, *74*
  secondary colours 74, 86
  shocking clashes – that work 86–7
  warm and cosy colours 82–3
colour cards 74
colour wheel 71, 74, 86
compact living 180–85
compost 198, 199, 200
computers 92, 142, *161*, 186, 192, *193*
concrete 104, 120, 172
Conran, Sir Terence 12, *12*, *14*, 16, 154, *163*, 175
cookers 124
cork 102, *105*, 197
cornices 172
Cornish Kitchenware 44
cotton 102, 197
Creimer, Matias *177*
crochet *101*
Crosland, Charlotte 76
Crosland, Neisha 76, *90*
cupboards 60, *63*, 88, 94, *102*, 124, 164
cups and saucers *33*, 88, 130
curtains 12, 30, 94, 102, 109, 150, 164
cushion covers 25, 30, 68, 109
cushions 71, 72, 78, 80, *82*, 88, *108*, 109, 142, 178
cutlery 112, 134
Czysz, Michael 71

D
Daily Mail Ideal Home Exhibition 176, *177*
David, Elizabeth *12*, 16
Day, Corinne 30
Day, Lucienne (née Conradi) 38, 46, 96, *97*
Day, Robin 38, 96, 107
Deaton, Charles 170, *170*, 178
deck chairs 148
decking *148*, 166
Demos *161*
denim 104
Design Museum, London 52
dining rooms 74, 118
Dish Doctor 34, *36*
dish drainers 34, *36*
display cabinets 60
displays *33*, 60, *61*
Dixon, Tom 6–7, *8*, 17–18, 38, 114, 172, 174, *174*, 192
Dockable Dwelling modular houses *177*
Doerfel, Nora 200, *200*
door handles 78
doormats 28
doors, sliding 166, 182, *188*
Dralon 71
dresses *25*, 26
Droog Design *54*
Dunster, Bill 194, *195*
Duralex 17, 138
dustbins (trash cans) 17, 34, *35*
dustpan-and-brush sets 25, 34, *35*
duvet covers 17, 25, 72, *98*
  Pixel *166*
duvets (continental quilts) 12, 30, *63*, 162, *163*, 184

E
Eames, Charles 46, 96, 107
Eames, Ray 96, 107
eco tips 198
ecological home 194–201
eco materials 196–7
  how to make your home more eco-friendly 198–9

Edelkoort, Li 172
eiderdowns *22*, 98
Eindhoven Design Academy 58
electrical ties 25
entrances 28, 74
espresso 130
  making 131
European Union 194, *195*
Evenhuis, Willeke 192, *193*
eyewear 58

F
fabrics *33*, 86, 92, 101, 105
fairy lights 26, 30, *31*, 148
farmers' markets 198
feather dusters 25
Featherstone, Sarah 152, *152*
felt *35*
Ferrero, J M *199*
Festival of Britain (1951) 12, 96
Finland 12
fireplaces 71, 104, 172
Fletcher, Alan 38, *39*, 40
flock 99
floors 102
  concrete 104
  eco-friendly 198
  limestone 102, 154
  mezzanine *184*
  stone 104
  wooden *35*, 102, 190
florals *90*, *98*, 99, 162
flowers 25, 30, *33*, *85*, 86, *134*
foil 114
France *12*, 16, 17
Fresh Fat plastic products 192, *193*
fur, fake 109
furniture *12*
  coordinated 150
  dark, heavy 12
  displayed *17*
  flat-pack 16
  'furniture while you wait' 25, 174, 192–3
  futuristic 170, 172
  Rough-and-Ready 58
  UP *174*
futons 160

G
Gabriel, Alex 192, *193*
Galileo Galilei 176
galvanized metal 17
Gamper, Martino 25, *27*
Gap, the, Clerkenwell, London 180
Gehry, Frank 197
Gervis, Heti 80, *80*
gingham 94
Giovannoni, Stefano 34
glass 16, 30, *33*, 71, 102, 105, 112, 113, 172, 197
glasses *12*, 16, 17, 134, 138
Gowans, Lucy 166, *166*
Grange, Kenneth 26, 40, *41*
Gray, Bethan 184
Gschwendter, Gitta 28, *28*
Guardian 43, 46

H
Habitat
  appeals to a wide range of shoppers 16
  Art on Demand scheme 174
  catalogues *16*, 17, *17*, 121
  first real 'lifestyle' store 16–17

Fulham Road store 12, 16
introduces the duvet to the UK 162
launch of (1964) 12, *14*
logo 16
name 16
a new concept on the British high street *12*
prices 18
range of products 18, 175
Tottenham Court Road store *18*
Hagan, Joe 180
hallways 28, *28*, 74, *90*
  furniture 28, *28*
  Hidden hallway unit 28, *28*
Harrison, George 16
Heals 96
hearths *82*, 124
Hecht, Sam 182
Hemingway, Gerardine 120
Hemingway, Wayne 120, 123
hessian (burlap) 104
high-rise living 180
Hirst, Damien 72
home offices 186, *188*
hooks 28, *28*, 34, 184
hot tubs 158, *158*
House Beautiful magazine *14*
House of the Future 176, *177*
Hulanicki, Barbara 16

I
Industrial Facility 182, *182*
Inflate *188*
internet 186
Italy 16

J
Jacobsen, Arne 46, 92
Jacuzzis 154, *158*
JAM *27*, 30
Japanese apartments 180, 182, *182*
Jerrentrup, Marco 128, *128*
Jones, Niki 92

K
Kandinsky, Wassily 96
Kartell 34, 65
Kenneth Grange Designs 40
Kenwood Chef food mixer 40
kimonos 26, 88
kitchen 72, 74, 94, *101*, *102*, *105*, *114*, 118, 120, 123, 124, *124*, 150, 154, 180, 182, *182*
  'Equipment' 182, *182*
kitchen steps 34
Kodak Instamatic camera 40
Kravitz, Lenny 71
Kvadrat 92

L
Lagerfeld, Karl 60
lambswool 109
lamps 12, 192
  Arcos 172, *172*
lampshades 17, 72, 88, 112, *121*, 164, 192, *193*
  Buona Sena *54*
  Garland 58, *59*
  Midsummer *59*
  Styrene 52, *54*
Latimer, Clive 46
laundry hampers 150
Le Corbusier 48, *172*
leather 38, 72, 172
  caring for 147
lemonade, easy homemade 148

Lévy, Catherine 30
lighting 16, 30, 52, 123, 154
lights 12, *30*, 52-9, 71
  Arcos lamp 172, *172*
  Bulb 52
  Eightfifty 52, *52*
  Mandarin light *43*
  mirror ball 174, *174*
  Watt 52
  Wednesday Light 58
limestone 102, 154
linoleum 198
living room 72, 74, *90*, 118, 120, 123, 142-5, *188*
Living Space of Tomorrow (Colani) 176
lofts 51, *102*, *114*, 118, 120, *172*, *188*
London 180
  black taxicab 40
Loos, Rachel 110, *110*
Lovag, Anti 178, *178*
Lutyens, Dominic 51, 51

M
McQueen, Alexander 58
Mad Max II (film) 170
magazine cuttings *71*, 88
Magis 34, *36*
magnetic board 28
mahogany 107
Manchester 180
  Museum of Science and Industry 52
mantelpiece 88
Marcel coat stand *51*
Marimekko 96
Marmoleum 102, 197
Massonnet, Henry 26, 40
Materialise 192, *193*
meals
  eating outdoors 140-41
  formal dining 134-5
  informal dining 136-7
  outdoor living 148, *148*
  the world in your bowl 132-3
Mebel 38
Memphis Group 51
Menuez, Ross 112
mezzanine floor *184*
Microflat 180, *180*
Milan Furniture Fair (2004) 182, *182*
milk bottles 25, *33*
Miró, Joan 96
mirror 28, *28*, *31*, 71, 105, 112, *113*, 154, 157
Miyake, Issey 197
mohair *108*
Mondrian, Piet 34, *74*
mood board 74, 86
mops 34
mosaic *101*, 154
Moss, Kate 30
mouldings 172
mugs 44
Muji *182*
Museum of Modern Art, New York 46, 130

N
napkins 134, 148
NASA *177*
Newson, Marc 34, *36*, 154
Norcross, Claire 52, *52*
nurseries 92, 123, 150

O
oak 102, 107
Office in a Bucket *188*

Op Art 92
open-plan living 118, 120, 166, 180, *188*
Optic prints (Panton) 92
optical illusions 92
Orange 186, *187*
Orange House of the Future 186, *187*
organization 61
Orwell, George: *A Nice Cup of Tea* 127
outdoor living 148-9
outdoor shower 158, *158*
ovens 124, 176, 182

P
paisley 98, *99*
panelling 82
Panton, Verner 38, 68, 71, *71*, 72, 92, *93*
paper 197
  Boule Japonaise 56, *57*
  doilies 25
  kites 26
  lanterns 57, 148
  Paper Mountain *199*
Parson, Tim 25-6
patchwork *101*
  quilts 30
patios *148*
pattern 88-101
  English eccentric 98-9
  geometric 92-3
  mixing and matching 100-101
  retro 96-7
Paulin, Pierre 38
Pawson, John 120
Pentagram 38, 40
pepper grinders 17, 138
Perspex 51, 61, *65*, 72, 112, *113*
Pesce, Gaetano 170, *174*
Philips 30
photo albums 92
photographs 61, 68, *71*, 88
Picasso, Pablo 34
picnics 140
picture frames 25, 86
pictures 88
Piercy Conner 180, *180*
pillowcases *98*
pillows *22*, *63*, 109
pine 107, 150
plastic 25, 34, 38, 40, 51, *65*, 71, 102, 105, 174, 192, *193*
plates *33*, 134
playroom 74, 118, 120, 150
playtime 150-51
plywood 28, 107, *107*
polyamide 192
polyester 102
polypropylene 46
polystyrene 52, *54*
polyurethane 170
porcelain 130
postcards 26, *33*, 88
Prébois, Sigolène 30
prints 12

Q
quilts 30, *33*, *98*, 109

R
Rabanne, Paco 172
rattan 104
recycling 194, 197, 198, *199*
Remy, Tejo *54*

ribbons 30
Riley, Bridget 92
Roget's Thesaurus 16
Rosenthal 96
rosewood 107
Royal College of Art, London 25, 38, 46, 58
rubber 102, 104, 157, 197, 198
rugs 71, 72, 78, *93*, 102, 105, 109, 142, 148
    Dart *110*
    washing a sheepskin rug 108

S
Saarinen, Eero 51
Sanderson Hotel, London 146
satin 30, 109
saucepans 25
saunas 154, 158, *158*
Scalextric track *150*
scrap metal 114
Sculptured House, Colorado (Jetson House) 170, *170*
seagrass 104
Selfridges department store, London 180, 192
Sellers, Peter 16
sequins 25, 30
sharing 118, 120, *121*
sheepskin *108*, 109, 142
sheets 17, 102, 162
shelving *28*, 88, 92, *101*, 112, 176, 184
Shepherd, Robert 34
Sherlock, George 25
shoe collection 60, *61*
shoe racks 28, *28*, 60
shopping bags *12*
showers 157
    outdoor 158, *158*
Shrimpton, Jean 16
sideboards 63
silk 25, 30, 102
Simpson, Ian 180
sinks 182, *182*
    twin 154, 157
SkyZED Flower Tower *195*
slate 102
sleep 160-61, 162
Sleeper (film) 170, *170*
slippers *35*, 142
Smith, Paul 92
Smithson, Alison 176, *177*
Smithson, Peter 176, *177*
sofas 30, *33*, 51, 72, *85*, 92, *108*, 109, 120, 142, *164*
    chesterfield 18, 146, *146*
    Forum leather 38
Soho House, New York 99
Solaire building, New York 194
spas 154, *154*
Spehl, Rainer 25, *27*
splashbacks 72, *114*
spoons, wooden *12*
spots 92, 101, 162
stainless steel 25, 72, 102, 112, 113, *113*
stairs *61*, *90*, 114
stairwells 120
Starck, Philippe 146, 154
steam rooms 154
stereos 176
Stirling prize (2003) 194
stools 63, 72
    Tam Tam 26, 40, *41*
storage 26, 28, *41*, 60-65, 180, 184
    pods 38
    units *27*, *101*, 184

stripes 92, 93, 101, *101*, 162
sugar pourers 126
sun loungers 148
    Teva Lounger *152*
Swarovski crystals 58
Sweden 12
swimming pool *113*
synthetics 102

T
tablecloths 12, 17, 88, 134, 148
    café 94-5
tables 192
    bedside 164
    coffee 51, 72, 92, 112, *136*, 142
    dining 17, 51, *121*
    folding 184
    glass 102
    how to lay a table 134
    kitchen 94, 123, 150
    monolithic *86*
    outdoors 148
    Perspex *113*
    Sonar coffee table 112
    and storage 63
    Surfer *190*
tableware 96
taffeta 102
tassels 30
Taylor, Pagan 16
tea-light holders 104
tea towels 25, 34, *35*
tea-making 127
teapots *12*, 88
    Brown Betty 18, 126
technology 186-9
television 118, 120, 124, 137, 142, *142*, *145*, *161*, 162, 176, 186, *187*
terracotta 102
tester pots 74
textiles *12*, 16, 68, 172
texture 71, 102-115
    hard and shiny 112-15
    rough and ready 104-5
    soft and cosy 108-9
Thomas Goodwin Green pottery, South Derbyshire 44
Thonet, Michael 48
throws 30, *33*, 72, 80, *80*, *98*, 109
Tilby, Paul 190, *190*
tiles 71, 72, *77*, 88, 94, 102, *105*, 154, 157
    photovoltaic *187*, 194, 198
toilet brush, Merdolino 34
toilets 154, 194
tongue-and-groove cladding 190
Top Cat cartoons 17, 34
towels 102, 154
toyboxes 150
TransGlass 30
trolley, Boby 178
trompe-l'oeil paint effects 88
Tsé & Tsé 30, *30*, *33*
Turner, Melinda Ashton 43, *43*
Twentieth-Century Legends Series 38, 39, 96
Twiggy 16
Tyvek paper *59*

U
underfloor heating 123, 154
Unity Peg 34, *35*
USE Architects 180

V
vacuum cleaners 25
vases 30, *33*, 78, 86, 88
vegetables, organic 198, *199*, 200
velvet 25, *25*, 30, 109
Victoria & Albert Museum, London: 'Brilliant' exhibition 52
viscose 102
Visiona 178
Visiona II 71
Vogue magazine 30

W
wallpaper 12, *33*, 68, *68*, *71*, 72, 76, 88, *97*, 99, 101
    Flamingo *90*, 99
    framing 92
    Hummingbird 99
    Rajapur 99
    striped *101*
walls
    Artexed 71
    brick 72, 104, *105*
    glossy 105
    knocking down 120, 184
    matt 105
    painted 68, 71-2, 86, *86*, 148, 150, 164, 172, 197
    painting vertical stripes 92
walnut 28, 107
washing machines 25, *27*, 180, 186, *187*
wenge 107
Westborough Primary School, Westcliff-on-Sea, Essex 197
wet rooms 157
Whirlpool Italia 182, *182*
whirlpools 154
Wichita House 178, *178*
wicker 104, 150
Wigglesworth, Sarah 194
Williamson, Matthew 86
wind turbines 198
window boxes 198
wine glasses 17
woks 132
    how to care for your wok 132
wood 72, 104, 107
wool 72, 102
wrapping paper 101

Y
Yale University School of Art 38
Yoshioka, Tokujin 180, *182*

habitat store directory
www.habitat.co.uk

Retail Stores

United Kingdom

Bath
1–4 New Bond Street
BA1 1BE
T +44 (0)1225 460 623
F +44 (0)1225 444 280

Batley
Redbrick Mill
218 Bradford Road
Batley Carr
West Yorkshire
WF17 6JF
T +44 (0)1924 468 960
F +44 (0)1924 469 881

Birmingham
88–91 New Street
B2 4HS
T +44 (0)121 643 5647
F +44 (0)121 643 5198

Bluewater
Unit 105
Upper Guild Hall
Bluewater, Greenhithe
DA9 9SS
T +44 (0)1322 387 162
F +44 (0)1322 624 234

Bournemouth
Parkway House
Avenue Road
BH2 5SL
T +44 (0)1202 291 011
F +44 (0)1202 292 080

Brighton
11 Churchill Square
Western Road
BN1 2EP
T +44 (0)1273 324 831
F +44 (0)1273 772 744

Bristol
Beacon House
Queens Road
Clifton BS8 1QY
T +44 (0)117 973 7012
F +44 (0)117 923 8439

Bromley
Hanover Place
44 High Street
BR1 1EJ
T +44 (0)208 466 8411
F +44 (0)208 313 0948

Cambridge
9–17 Fitzroy Street
CB1 1ER
T +44 (0)1223 323 644
F +44 (0)1223 464 185

Canterbury
St Andrews Close
Rheims Way
CT1 2RL
T +44 (0)1227 450 808
F +44 (0)1227 456 012

Cardiff
9–11 The Hayes Building
The Hayes
CF10 1AH
T +44 (0)2920 228 811
F +44 (0)2920 225 441

Chelmsford
1-5 Grays Brewery Yard
Springfield Road
CM2 6QR
T +44 (0)1245 359 033
F +44 (0)1245 490 767

Cheltenham
108–110 The
Promenade
GL50 1NL
T +44 (0)1242 234 231
F +44 (0)1242 224 930

Chester
Newgate
Pepper Street
CH1 1DX
T +44 (0)1244 313 014
F +44 (0)1244 315 178

Edinburgh
32 Shandwick Place
EH2 4RT
T +44 (0)131 225 9151
F +44 (0)131 220 3737

Exeter
21–22 Queen Street
EX4 3SH
T +44 (0)1392 254 000
F +44 (0)1392 421 564

Glasgow
Unit 1–3
The Pinnacle Building
160 Bothwell Street
G2 7EA
T +44 (0)141 248 2517
F +44 (0)141 222 2478

Guildford
149 High Street
GU1 3AD
T +44 (0)1483 451 345
F +44 (0)1483 451 354

Harrogate
57-59 Station Parade
HG1 1TT
T +44 (0)1423 526 788
F +44 (0)1423 531 447

Hatfield
Oldings Corner
Comet Way
AL9 5JU
T +44 (0)01707 275671
F +44 (0)1707 269 361

Kingston
14–16 Eden Walk
KT1 1BP
T +44 (0)208 547 3929
F +44 (0)208 547 1944

Leeds
38 Briggate
LS1 5YN
T +44 (0)113 244 9036
F +44 (0)113 242 8654

Leicester
40-50 High Street
LE1 5YN
T +44 (0)116 291 3777
F +44 (0)116 291 3778

London NW3
191–217 Finchley Road
NW3 6NW
T +44 (0)207 328 3444
F +44 (0)207 328 3596

London W6
19–20 Kings Mall
Hammersmith
W6 0PZ
T +44 (0)208 741 7111
F +44 (0)208 741 1826

London W8
26-40 Kensington
High Street
W8 4PF
T +44 (0)20 7795 6055
F +44 (0)20 7376 2615

London SW3
208 Kings Road
SW3 5XP
T +44 (0)207 351 1211
F +44 (0)207 351 4249

London W1
196 Tottenham
Court Road
W1P 9LD
T +44 (0)207 631 3880
F +44 (0)207 631 1322

Maidenhead
Bishops Centre
Bath Road
SL6 0QB
T +44 (0)1628 664 514
F +44 (0)1628 664 090

Manchester
11–16 St Ann Street
M2 7LG
T +44 (0)161 835 3612
F +44 (0)161 835 3620

Manchester South
Southmoor Road
Wythenshawe
M23 9LR
T +44 (0)161 902 0441
F +44 (0)161 946 0569

Milton Keynes
Central Retail Park
Patriot Drive
Rooksley
MK13 8PU
T +44 (0)1908 696 482
F +44 (0)1908 696 476

Norwich
13-25 London Street
NR2 1JD
T +44 (0)1603 665 981
F +44 (0)1603 616 242

Nottingham
Units 1–2
54-57 Long Row West
NG1 6JB
T +44 (0)115 950 9943
F +44 (0)115 958 1654

Oxford
Seacourt Tower
West Way
Botley OX2 0JJ
T +44 (0)1865 790 313
F +44 (0)1865 790 317

Richmond
18-20 George Street
TW9 1JW
T +44 (0)208 332 9226
F +44 (0)208 948 2544

Solihull
Sears Retail Park
Oakenshaw Road
Shirley
West Midlands
B90 4QY
T +44 (0)121 733 2579
F +44 (0)121 733 6038

Southampton
Unit MSU4
West Quay Shopping
Centre
45 Above Bar
Hampshire
SO15 1QE
T +44 (0)2380 632 846
F +44 (0)2380 632 846

Tunbridge Wells
95-97 Mount
Pleasant Road
TN1 1QG
T +44 (0)1892 544 066
F +44 (0)1892 536 623

York
26-27 High Ousegate
YO1 8RX
T +44 (0)1904 659 368
F +44 (0)1904 612 412